Virtues
of
Leadership

WILLIAM J. BENNETT

W PUBLISHING GROUP
www.wpublishinggroup.com

A Division of Thomas Nelson, Inc.
www.ThomasNelson.com

Virtues of Leadership

© 2001 W Publishing Group

Published by W Publishing Group, a Division of Thomas Nelson, Inc., P.O. Box 141000, Nashville, Tennessee 37214. All rights reserved. No portion of this book may be reproduced, stored in a retrieval system, or transmitted in any form or by any means—electronic, mechanical, photocopy, recording, or any other—except for brief quotations in printed reviews, without the prior permission of the publisher.

Material in this book is compiled from both *The Book of Virtues* and *The Moral Compass* by William J. Bennett, copyright © 1993 by William J Bennett and copyright © 1996 by William J. Bennett.

Published by arrangement with Simon & Shuster, Inc.

Library of Congress Cataloging-in-Publication Data

ISBN 0–8499–1717–4

Printed in the United States of America

01 02 03 04 05 06 07 08 09 — 9 8 7 6 5 4 3 2 1

Contents

Introduction

WILLIAM J. BENNETT

T here are moments in life that test mettle and reveal quali-
ties of leadership. For the Rev. Martin Luther King, Jr.,
one of those moments came on a January night in 1956. King
had left his wife and baby at their home in Montgomery,
Alabama, to go to a meeting at a nearby church. As the meeting wound down, someone rushed in with dreadful news: "Your
house has been bombed."

King raced home and pushed his way through the crowd
gathering on his lawn. The bomb had exploded on the front
porch and sent glass flying into the living room. By now the
house was full of people. King forced his way inside and found
his family safe.

Outside, however, trouble was brewing. The crowd was
angry. They wanted revenge against whomever had done this
terrible thing. Some people carried guns and broken bottles.
They began jeering and shouting at the policemen. The situation was about to spin out of control. That's when King stepped
onto his porch.

Silence fell over the crowd. Suddenly everything was perfectly still.

King told them in a calm voice that his wife and daughter were all right. "I want you to go home and put down your weapons," he said. He told them they could not solve their problems with violence. That would only harm their cause. He reminded them of the teachings of the Bible: "We must meet hate with love."

Then something amazing happened. "Amen," someone said. "God bless you," others called. The crowd, which a moment ago had been on the verge of bloodshed, began to drift apart. A night that had been on the verge of chaos came to a quiet, if uneasy, close. Pictures of King urging calm from his shattered porch made newspapers across the country, and support for the civil rights movement swelled.

What made those people so willing to listen to King at that fragile moment? What made the greatest part of a nation want to follow him? It was no one thing, of course, but a mixture— a mixture of vision and talent and, not the least, virtue. This man of God had truth and right on his side, and he possessed a store of traits such as compassion, perseverance, courage, wisdom, and faith. These things make up a man or woman people want to follow.

Most of us never have to face such high stakes. But all of us, at certain times in our lives, are called to lead in some capacity: as team captain, club president, state representative, or member of a student council, vestry, or board of directors. This book reminds us of the virtues required to hold these positions. In these selections, we see that leaders are ultimately judged in terms of how well they serve their followers and by the examples they set. They lead not just by command but by the force of good character. And we notice that before they lead, they learn to be good followers—they know how to help shoulder a load and share hardships.

Dwight D. Eisenhower once observed that "a platoon leader doesn't get his platoon to go by getting up and shouting, 'I am smarter! I am bigger! I am stronger! I am the leader!' He gets men to go along with him because they want to do it for him and they believe in him."

Getting others to believe in you—that's no easy task. If we want to be good leaders, we can begin by looking in these pages to see how others have done it.

The Birds Who Befriended a King

ADAPTED FROM A RETELLING
BY CONSTANCE ARMFIELD

*"And men came from all peoples to hear the wisdom of Solomon,"
the first book of Kings in the Bible tells us. No leader in history has
been more renowned for learning and judgment than the tenth-century
B.C. ruler of Israel and Judah. Every boy or girl who hopes someday to
lead a company, community, or country would do well to learn the les-
son Solomon learns in this story: To lead is to serve.*

*The hoopoes in the story below are jay-sized birds living in Africa,
in India, and in warm, dry regions of southern Europe. Because of its
striking plumage, including a showy crown of feathers, the hoopoe is a
favorite bird of folklore.*

Once the great King Solomon was journeying in the desert.
Across the sand the king's caravan made its way, the
camels' embroidered saddlecloths as bright as flowers, and their
jeweled bridles flashing as brightly as the sun itself. But the heat
smote down on the king's head, and Solomon yearned for

shade. As if in answer to his longing, who should appear but a flock of Hoopoes? Being curious by nature, they circled around until they reached the king's camel and kept just overhead, so that they might watch this most famous of all monarchs and perhaps overhear some word of wisdom.

Thus the little birds cast a grateful shadow over the king for his whole journey. And richly repaid they were. For Solomon, who was always polite to the humblest creature in his kingdom, conversed freely with them the whole time, bestowing upon them many wise words. When they reached his palace, he thanked them for providing the shade, and asked what he could do in return.

Now the Hoopoes had begun their conversation with Solomon modestly enough; in fact, they had been very surprised that he had spoken to them at all. But he had questioned them so kindly about their way of living, and their likes and preferences and relations, that they lost their fear of him. They came into his wonderful palace and saw all the servants in their shining robes standing behind the king's throne, and waiting on his table, and lining the great courtyard. They beheld the walls of ivory inlaid with gold, and the golden lions guarding the steps, and the white peacocks on their silver terraces. And it quite turned the little birds' heads to think they had journeyed right across the desert with the owner of all these riches.

So instead of answering Solomon with thanks on their part and telling him his words of wisdom were rich reward for any shelter they had given, the Hoopoes begged leave to consult together and withdrew to the palace roof, where they discussed what they would ask for.

Finally they decided they would like golden crowns such as the king himself wore; then they could return to the other birds and reign over them. At once the little birds flew down with a rush and made their request to the king as he walked in his wonderful garden.

"What the king has said, the king has said," Solomon replied. "The gift you desire shall be granted. Yet, because you rendered me true service, when you wish to get rid of your crowns, you may return and exchange them for wisdom."

"Nay, king," said the Hoopoes. "Well we know that wisdom has brought you great renown, but no one would bow down to you or give attention to your words, unless you wore your golden crown. We shall be able to repeat your wise words profitably now, for all will listen when they see gold crowns on our heads, too."

"All the same, return to me without fear or shame, if your crowns do not satisfy," said King Solomon kindly. Then he ordered his goldsmiths to supply the Hoopoes with crowns of the finest gold. Off flew the silly birds, with the shining crowns upon their heads, prouder than peacocks and chattering more loudly than parrots.

They could scarcely wait to get back to their friends and hear their exclamations. But when the Hoopoes announced they were now Kings of the Bird World, their friends only laughed and said they were quite satisfied with Solomon, and he was the only king they wished or needed. Then they drove the Hoopoes from the trees, for their golden crowns were always catching in the branches, and the other birds grew tired of freeing them. But the Hoopoes decided the other birds were only jealous and, rather flattered, gathered around the pools so they could admire themselves in the water.

Very soon people began to notice the antics of the silly little things as they strutted up and down, cocking their heads first this way, then that. Finally a man caught one and discovered the wonderful gold crown it wore. He hurried off to a goldsmith, who gave him a high price for it. The man rushed back to the pool and laid snares for the Hoopoes, who were so taken up with admiring themselves that they walked straight into the traps.

Then came the saddest time for the Hoopoes. Everyone began to hunt them. The poor little birds could not go to the wells and the pools, for they were thick with nets. They could not go into the gardens, for fowlers lurked behind the flowers. They could not fly up onto the housetops, for even there the people had set traps for them. There was not a spot on earth where they could rest. At last the wretched little birds flew back to the palace and waited until they beheld the great King Solomon coming along his terrace, listening to his singers as they performed in the cool of the evening.

"O king," they said, "we have found that golden crowns are vanity. We know not what you do to keep yourself from being chased about and hunted, and so we have come to ask you to remove ours from us."

"Beloved Hoopoes," said the king, "a crown that people are expected to bow down to always sits heavy on the head, and a crown that excites envy is a net for the feet. The only crown that can be worn with comfort is the crown of service, and that crown should spring up naturally so that no one takes any particular notice of it."

"Give us that crown of service, O wise king," said the poor little Hoopoes very humbly, for they now wanted nothing better than to live without notice.

"May it shelter you even as it sheltered me," said the great king; and on their heads, the Hoopoes beheld crowns of feathers. But with these crowns came quite a new feeling to the Hoopoes. They no longer wished to rule, but to serve.

Brotherhood of Long Ago

FANNY E. COE

Here is a story of perseverance winning the day because a leader knew how to help shoulder the load. This act of encouragement and compassion by the Marquis de Lafayette (1757–1834) reminds us of the story of Saint Martin.

More than two hundred years ago, when our country was fighting against England, there came to help us a young French nobleman named Lafayette. Although only a boy of nineteen years, he had run away from his country because he longed to fight for liberty. He said that he came to learn, not to teach, and, from the first, he took George Washington for an ideal.

Lafayette and Washington became lifelong friends. Lafayette named his son for Washington and, on his return to America in 1787, he paid a delightful visit to Washington at Mount Vernon. He promised soon to return, but almost forty years passed by before he kept his word.

He came at last, in 1824, a bent old man, with a heart loyal as ever to his adopted country. He visited every state and territory in the Union and was welcomed everywhere with the warmest enthusiasm. Receptions, dinner parties, and balls followed each other in brilliant succession, always with Lafayette the chief figure. The welcome of the people was voiced in a song of the time:

> "But our hearts, Lafayette,
> We bow not the neck,
> We bend not the knee,
> But our hearts, Lafayette,
> We surrender to thee."

The following incident occurred during the visit of 1824.

A brilliant reception was under way. A slowly moving line of stately guests passed by the noble old marquis, who greeted each with courtly grace. Presently there approached an old soldier clad in a worn Continental uniform. In his hand was an ancient musket, and across his shoulder was thrown a small blanket, or rather a piece of blanket. On reaching the marquis, the veteran drew himself up in the stiff fashion of the old-time drill and gave the military salute. As Lafayette returned the salute, tears sprang to his eyes. The tattered uniform, the ancient flintlock, the silver-haired veteran, even older than himself, recalled the dear past.

"Do you know me?" asked the soldier. Lafayette's manner had led him to think himself personally remembered.

"Indeed, I cannot say that I do," was the frank reply.

"Do you remember the frosts and snows of Valley Forge?"

"I shall never forget them," answered Lafayette.

"One bitter night, General Lafayette, you were going the rounds at Valley Forge. You came upon a sentry in thin clothing and without stockings. He was slowly freezing to death. You took his musket, saying, 'Go to my hut. There you will find stockings, a blanket, and a fire. After warming yourself, bring the blanket to me. Meanwhile I will keep guard.'

"The soldier obeyed directions. When he returned to his post, you, General Lafayette, cut the blanket in two. One half you kept, the other you presented to the sentry. Here, General, is one half of that blanket, for I am the sentry whose life you saved."

The Character of Leadership

THOMAS JEFFERSON

Here is one great American leader writing honestly and unselfishly about another. Here is a true portrait of the character of leadership. Jefferson wrote this probing, candid assessment at Monticello in a letter to Dr. Walter Jones dated January 2, 1814.

I think I knew General Washington intimately and thoroughly; and were I called on to delineate his character, it should be in terms like these.

His mind was great and powerful, without being of the very first order; his penetration strong, though not so acute as that of a Newton, Bacon, or Locke; and as far as he saw, no judgment was ever sounder. It was slow in operation, being little aided by invention or imagination, but sure in conclusion. Hence the common remark of his officers, of the advantage he derived from councils of war, where hearing all suggestions, he selected whatever was best; and certainly no general ever planned his battles more judiciously. But if deranged during the course of the action, if any member of his plan was dislocated by sudden circumstances, he was slow in readjustment. The consequence was, that he often failed in the field, and rarely against an enemy in station, as at Boston and York. He was incapable of fear, meeting personal dangers with the calmest unconcern. Perhaps the strongest feature in his character was prudence, never acting until every circumstance, every consideration, was maturely weighed; refraining if he saw a doubt, but, when once decided, going through with his purpose, whatever obstacles opposed. His integrity was most pure, his justice the most inflexible I have ever known, no motives of interest or consanguinity, of friendship or hatred, being able to bias his decision. He was, indeed, in every sense of the words, a wise, a good, and a great man. His temper was naturally irritable and high toned; but reflection and resolution had obtained a firm and habitual ascendancy over it. If ever, however, it broke its bonds, he was most tremendous in his wrath. In his expenses he was honorable, but exact; liberal in contributions to whatever promised utility; but frowning and unyielding on all visionary projects, and all unworthy calls on his charity. His heart was not warm in its affections; but he exactly calculated every man's value, and gave him a solid esteem proportioned to it.

His person, you know, was fine, his stature exactly what one would wish, his deportment easy, erect, and noble; the best horseman of his age, and the most graceful figure that could be seen on horseback. Although in the circle of his friends, where he might be unreserved with safety, he took a free share in conversation, his colloquial talents were not above mediocrity, possessing neither copiousness of ideas, nor fluency of words. In public, when called on for a sudden opinion, he was unready, short, and embarrassed. Yet he wrote readily, rather diffusely, in an easy and correct style. This he had acquired by conversation with the world, for his education was merely reading, writing, and common arithmetic, to which he added surveying at a later day. His time was employed in action chiefly, reading little, and that only in agriculture and English history. His correspondence became necessarily extensive, and, with journalizing his agricultural proceedings, occupied most of his leisure hours within doors. On the whole, his character was, in its mass, perfect, in nothing bad, in few points indifferent; and it may truly be said, that never did nature and fortune combine more perfectly to make a man great, and to place him in the same constellation with whatever worthies have merited from man an everlasting remembrance.

For his was the singular destiny and merit, of leading the armies of his country successfully through an arduous war, for the establishment of its independence; of conducting its councils through the birth of a government, new in its forms and principles, until it had settled down into a quiet and orderly train; and of scrupulously obeying the laws through the whole of his career, civil and military, of which the history of the world furnishes no other example.

Charlemagne and the Robber Knight

ADAPTED FROM A RETELLING
BY MARIE FRARY AND CHARLES STEBBINS

In this old German legend we find true force of character—the kind that leads by example, pulling others upward. Charlemagne (742–814), also known as Charles the First, king of France and emperor of the Holy Roman Empire, established a cultural revival that laid the foundation of European civilization in the late Middle Ages.

O nce the great King Charlemagne built a magnificent palace on the river Rhine, where he could watch the waters slip past, and gaze on the distant hills, and hunt with his friends in the deep, green forests. When the castle was completed he went to visit it. The very first night he slept there, an angel appeared in his dreams. It stood by his bed, clothed in splendid light, and said: "Arise, good Emperor. Arise, go forth secretly, and steal."

Charlemagne woke, much puzzled at the dream. It seemed impossible that an emperor should be ordered to become a robber. So he lay down and went back to sleep.

But the angel reappeared again. "Arise, Emperor," it said. "Go forth, and steal from your own people."

Again Charlemagne woke, aghast at the command. He still could not believe such an order could come from an angel, so he did not move. Once more the angel appeared by the side of his bed. It stretched forth its hand, saying: "Arise! Do not tarry. Go into the forest and steal, or repent forever."

Charlemagne rose and passed quietly through the halls of his castle. His knights were fast asleep. He went to his stable, saddled his horse, armed himself, and rode silently into the depths of the forest.

As he was going along the dark way thoughtfully, he heard someone approaching, and he soon perceived it was a knight clad in black armor. Charlemagne could think of no good reason why a knight should be riding at such an hour, so he challenged the man.

"Where are you riding, and upon what mission, at this time of the night?" he demanded.

The knight did not answer, but put spurs to his horse and charged the Emperor. Seeing his movement, the Emperor did likewise, and the two met with a violent shock. Both were unhorsed, and in the hand-to-hand conflict which followed, the Emperor got the better of the unknown knight and brought him to the ground. With his sword at the stranger's throat, he demanded his name.

"I am Elbegast," he replied, "the robber knight, who has committed many a bold deed. You are the first who has had the power to overcome me."

"Arise," said the Emperor, without revealing who he was, "and come with me. I am on a mission like thine own."

Without hesitating, the robber knight joined his conqueror. They rode through the forest until they reached a stately house. It was the home of Arnot, one of the Emperor's most trusted ministers.

Elbegast was not long in gaining entrance. Bidding his companion to wait for him outside, he stole noiselessly into the house.

As he approached the minister's bedroom, the sound of voices in earnest conversation came to his ears. He listened, and heard Arnot disclose to his wife a plan for the murder of the Emperor himself on the following day.

Forgetting his purpose for breaking into the house, the knight made his way hastily back to his companion, and begged him to go at once to Charlemagne and inform him of the coming danger.

"Why not go yourself and tell him?" asked the Emperor.

Elbegast hung his head.

"I would gladly do it, if I could. A man like me, who has committed evil deeds, dares not seek out the Emperor. I would risk imprisonment to save his life, but it would do no good— the Emperor would scarcely believe a man with my reputation. But I tell you this: Whatever I have done, I hold great admiration for the man who has never been conquered in battle, and who has always worked for the good of his people. He rules wisely and kindly, and I would keep him from harm."

Then Charlemagne and Elbegast parted, one returning to his stronghold in the mountains and the other retracing his steps slowly and thoughtfully to his palace.

On the morrow Arnot and his conspirators attempted to carry out their plans, but the Emperor was ready for them. As they came riding into the castle courtyard, the gates slammed shut behind them, and a dozen guards sprang forth.

"What kind of greeting is this for someone who has come to pay his respects to his emperor?" Arnot demanded, with pretended indignation.

"What kind of greeting do you bring, when you come to pay your respects this way?" asked one of the guards. As he spoke, he tore the clothes of Arnot and his companions, disclosing their hidden daggers.

Charlemagne took all of them into custody, and they confessed their plot against him.

The Emperor then set his mind upon Elbegast. He sent a messenger to him, requesting him to come to the palace.

"I, Charlemagne, Emperor of Germany," his message ran, "would speak privately with Elbegast, the robber knight, and promise him safe conduct to and from my castle."

Elbegast rode to the palace and was admitted to the private council chamber. Soon a man entered, clad in armor, and Elbegast recognized the knight who had been his companion the night before.

"Elbegast," said Charlemagne, "you recognize me and yet you do not know me."

Then Charlemagne raised his visor, and the robber knight saw that he was standing in the presence of the Emperor.

"You have done wrong in the past," said Charlemagne. "But now you have done me faithful duty. Here is your chance to begin your life anew. I offer you a place among my retainers. A

man of your courage and loyalty is worthy of a place in the
Emperor's service."

Elbegast was so moved that he could hardly speak.
Charlemagne was the only man who had ever been able to
defeat him in battle, and for this he admired him greatly. But
more than this, he stood in awe of the Emperor's reputation for
kindness and wisdom. And so Elbegast, the robber knight, was
disarmed by Charlemagne's own character. He willingly forsook
his evil life in the forest and became a devoted friend to the end
of his days.

And in commemoration of the angel's visit, which had
caused him to find this loyal knight, Charlemagne named his
new castle Ingelheim, meaning "angel's home."

The Conscience of the Nation Must Be Roused

FREDERICK DOUGLASS

Frederick Douglass was born a slave in 1817 and raised by his grandmother on a Maryland plantation until sent to work at age eight in Baltimore. There, with the help of his new master's wife, he began to educate himself, an activity forbidden by law. In 1838, he escaped and settled in New Bedford, Massachusetts, and began working for the antislavery cause. It was not long before he was the nation's leading black abolitionist and one of its most brilliant orators.

In 1852, having been invited to deliver an Independence Day address in Rochester, New York, Douglass seized the occasion to hold the "scorching iron" of moral reproach to the nation's conscience. For Douglass and all black Americans, the Fourth of July was not an anniversary on which to rejoice at the rights and freedoms conferred by democracy; it was a day of deepest shame for those betraying the most basic moral obligations toward their fellowmen. Here is a brave soul holding America accountable for its sins.

F ellow citizens, pardon me, allow me to ask, why am I called upon to speak here today? What have I, or those I represent, to do with your national independence? Are the great principles of political freedom and of natural justice, embodied in that Declaration of Independence, extended to us? And am I, therefore, called upon to bring our humble offering to the national altar, and to confess the benefits and express devout gratitude for the blessings resulting from your independence to us?

Would to God, both for your sakes and ours, that an affirmative answer could be truthfully returned to these questions! . . .

But such is not the state of the case. I say it with a sad sense of the disparity between us. I am not included within the pale of this glorious anniversary! Your high independence only reveals the immeasurable distance between us. The blessings in which you, this day, rejoice are not enjoyed in common. The rich inheritance of justice, liberty, prosperity, and independence bequeathed by your fathers is shared by you, not by me. The sunlight that brought light and healing to you has brought stripes and death to me. This Fourth of July is yours, not mine. You may rejoice, I must mourn. To drag a man in fetters into the grand illuminated temple of liberty, and call upon him to join you in joyous anthems, were inhuman mockery and sacrilegious irony. . . .

Fellow citizens, above your national, tumultuous joy, I hear the mournful wail of millions! Whose chains, heavy and grievous yesterday, are, today, rendered more intolerable by the jubilee shouts that reach them. If I do forget, if I do not faithfully remember those bleeding children of sorrow this day, "may my right hand forget her cunning, and may my tongue cleave to the roof of my mouth!" To forget them, to pass lightly over their wrongs, and to chime in with the popular theme would be treason most scandalous and shocking, and would make me a reproach before God and the world. My subject, then, fellow citizens, is *American slavery.* I shall see this day and its popular characteristics from the slave's point of view. Standing there identified with the American bondman, making his wrongs mine, I do not hesitate to declare with all my soul that the character and conduct of this nation never looked blacker to me than on this Fourth of July! Whether we turn to the declarations of the past or to the professions of the present, the conduct of the nation seems equally hideous and revolting. America is false to the past, false to the present, and solemnly binds herself to be false to the future. Standing with God and the crushed and bleeding slave on this occasion, I will, in the name of humanity which is outraged, in the name of liberty which is fettered, in the name of the Constitution and the Bible which are disregarded and trampled upon, dare to call in question and to denounce, with all the emphasis I can command, everything that serves to perpetuate slavery—the great sin and shame of America! . . .

What, am I to argue that it is wrong to make men brutes, to rob them of their liberty, to work them without wages, to keep them ignorant of their relations to their fellowmen, to beat them with sticks, to flay their flesh with the lash, to load their limbs with irons, to hunt them with dogs, to sell them at auction, to sunder their families, to knock out their teeth, to burn their flesh, to starve them into obedience and submission to their masters? Must I argue that a system thus marked with blood, and stained with pollution, is wrong? No! I will not. I have better employment for my time and strength than such arguments would imply.

What, then, remains to be argued? Is it that slavery is not divine; that God did not establish it; that our doctors of divinity are mistaken? There is blasphemy in the thought. That which is inhuman cannot be divine! Who can reason on such a proposition? They that can may; I cannot. The time for such argument is past.

At a time like this, scorching iron, not convincing argument, is needed. O! had I the ability, and could I reach the nation's ear, I would today pour out a fiery stream of biting ridicule, blasting reproach, withering sarcasm, and stern rebuke. For it is not light that is needed, but fire; it is not the gentle shower, but thunder. We need the storm, the whirlwind, and the earthquake. The feeling of the nation must be quickened; the conscience of the nation must be roused; the propriety of the nation must be startled; the hypocrisy of the nation must be exposed; and its crimes against God and man must be proclaimed and denounced.

What, to the American slave, is your Fourth of July? I answer: a day that reveals to him, more than all other days in the year, the gross injustice and cruelty to which he is the constant victim. To him, your celebration is a sham; your boasted liberty, an unholy license; your national greatness, swelling vanity; your sounds of rejoicing are empty and heartless; your denunciation of tyrants, brass-fronted impudence; your shouts of liberty and equality, hollow mockery; your prayers and hymns, your sermons and thanksgivings, with all your religious parade and solemnity, are, to Him, mere bombast, fraud, deception, impiety, and hypocrisy—a thin veil to cover up crimes which would disgrace a nation of savages. There is not a nation of savages, there is not a nation on the earth guilty of practices more shocking and bloody than are the people of the United States at this very hour.

Gideon and His Brave Three Hundred

ADAPTED FROM A RETELLING
BY FRANCES DADMUN AND JESSE LYMAN
HURLBUT

As this story from the book of Judges in the Bible reminds us, an important part of leadership is knowing how to choose the right people to lead. The story shows us how to look for courage and resolution and reminds us that it's not the size of the dog in the fight that counts, but the size of the fight in the dog.

Long ago, a young man lived in Israel whose name was Gideon. He was the only son his father had left. His brothers, older than he, had died in battle. For Israel was hard-pressed by the tribe of Midianites, who lived across the river Jordan. For a time they would lie quiet and Israel would think all was well; but as soon as the wheat fields of Israel were yellow and ripe for harvest, the Midianites would cross the river, fight with Israel, and carry off the wheat. Israel had been beaten so many times that now she dared not stir. Her men lived in caves, just as animals creep into holes in the earth to protect themselves.

Gideon thought it a shame. He was brave, too brave to hide in the earth and let the Midianites carry off his father's wheat. Then God put the thought in his heart to save his people. So it happened that one morning, when a frightened messenger came running to say that the Midianites had crossed the river again, Gideon stood on a hilltop and blew a trumpet.

The Israelites ran from their caves at the sound of the trumpet blast, and gathered around Gideon. Then he sent messengers throughout the land to call the fighting men together. The Israelites were so glad to have a brave leader that Gideon soon had an army of thirty-two thousand men.

Early in the morning they pitched their tents south of the enemy. When the Midianites woke and came out of their own tents, they stared in surprise. There was Israel just opposite, and from the number of tents, it looked like a great host!

But Gideon was not sure of his army. The men had been brave enough at the call of the trumpet, but when they faced the camp of the Midianites, extending up and down the valley as far as they could see, they began to wish they had stayed hidden in their own caves. They were not as sure as Gideon was that God would give them the victory. After all, they said to one another, what sort of captain was Gideon? He was little more than a boy.

But God said to Gideon: "Your army is too large. Send home all those who are afraid to fight."

And Gideon saw that a small army of brave men would be better than a multitude of cowards. So he sent word through the camp that whoever was afraid of the enemy should go home. Twenty-two thousand people went away, leaving only ten thousand in Gideon's army.

But God said to Gideon: "These people are yet too many. You need only a few of the bravest and best men to fight in this battle. Bring the men down the mountain, beside the water, and there I will show you how to find the ones you need."

So in the morning, by God's command, Gideon called his ten thousand men out and made them march down the hill, just as though they were going to attack the enemy. And when they were beside the water, he noticed how they drank, and set them apart into two companies.

As they came to the water, most of the men threw aside their shields and spears and knelt down to scoop up a drink with both hands together like a cup. If there had been any Midianites hidden in the bushes, they could have shot the drinkers with arrows, for they were off their guard. These men Gideon commanded to stand in one company.

But there were a few men who did not stop to take a long drink of water. Holding spear and shield in one hand, with eyes wide open in case the enemy should suddenly appear, they merely caught up a handful of water in passing and marched on, lapping the water from the other hand.

God said to Gideon: "Set by themselves these men who have lapped up each a handful of water. These are the ones I have chosen to set Israel free."

Gideon counted these men and found there were only three hundred. But they were three hundred earnest men, of one purpose, who would not turn aside from their aim, even to drink.

Gideon waited for the sun to go down. When it was dark, he crept into the camp of the Midianites, and listened. When he heard them talking, he was glad, for he could tell that the Midianites, for all their number, were afraid of the Israelites. So he hurried back to his own camp.

Gideon's plan did not need a large army, but it did need a few careful, bold men who would do exactly as their leader commanded. He gave to each of his three hundred soldiers a lamp, a pitcher, and a trumpet, and told the men what to do with them. The lamps were lighted, but were placed inside the pitchers, so they could not be seen. He divided his men into three companies and very quietly led them down the mountain in the middle of the night, and arranged them all around the Midianite camp.

Then at once a great shout rang out in the darkness, and after it came a crash of breaking pitchers and then a flash of light in every direction. The men blew their trumpets with a mighty noise. The Midianites were startled from their sleep to see enemies all around them, lights beaming and swords flashing in the darkness, and everywhere the sharp blaring of horns.

They were filled with sudden terror and thought only of escape, not of fighting. But wherever they turned, their enemies seemed to be standing with swords drawn. Their own land was east, across the river Jordan, and they fled in that direction, down a valley between the mountains, and they never came back again.

And so Israel was free, all because Gideon was brave and found three hundred men who stood with him.

Good King Wenceslas

BOHEMIAN FOLKTALE

Saint Wenceslas was a tenth-century duke of Bohemia. This old carol about him tells a beautiful legend that has come down to us from the Middle Ages. The incident is said to have taken place on Saint Stephen's Day, the day after Christmas. Wenceslas was standing at his castle window when he saw a figure struggling through the snow. The king and his young page set out to aid the man, but the boy's courage began to fail in the fierce blizzard. Wenceslas gently told him to walk close behind him, and it was then that the miracle occurred: The page found that green grass sprang up in the kindhearted monarch's footprints, and that as long as he placed his feet in the track, he seemed to be walking in the warmth of a summer's afternoon.

Good leaders bring others along in their footsteps, teaching by example.

Good King Wenceslas looked out
    On the Feast of Stephen,
When the snow lay round about,
    Deep, and crisp, and even.
Brightly shone the moon that night,
    Though the frost was cruel,
When a poor man came in sight,
    Gath'ring winter fuel.

"Hither, page, and stand by me,
    If thou know'st it, telling,
Yonder peasant, who is he?
    Where and what his dwelling?"
"Sire, he lives a good league hence,
    Underneath the mountain;
Right against the forest fence,
    By Saint Agnes's fountain."

"Bring me flesh, and bring me wine,
    Bring me pine logs hither:
Thou and I will see him dine,
    When we bear them thither."
Page and monarch forth they went,
    Forth they went together;
Through the rude wind's wild lament
    And the bitter weather.

"Sire, the night is darker now,
    And the wind blows stronger;
Fails my heart, I know not how,
    I can go no longer."
"Mark my footsteps, my good page;
    Tread thou in them boldly:
Thou shalt find the winter's rage
    Freeze thy blood less coldly."

In his master's steps he trod,
    Where the snow lay dinted;
Heat was in the very sod
    Which the saint had printed.
Therefore, Christian man, be sure,
    Wealth or rank possessing,
Ye who now will bless the poor,
    Shall yourselves find blessing.

The Gordian Knot

ADAPTED FROM A RETELLING
BY JAMES BALDWIN

Often leaders are people who aren't discouraged by the odds, who find a way through no matter what. This old story of determination and decisiveness is great to remember at times when you need to cut through red tape.

In the western part of Asia there is a rich and beautiful region which in olden times was called Phrygia. The people of that place once had a king named Gordius, a man who brought peace to the land by ruling wisely, righting old wrongs, and making laws for the good of all.

Now, when he became king, Gordius did something very strange and marvelous. In the temple of Jupiter overlooking the town, he tied a great knot of rope. So intricate were its twists and turns, and so deftly did Gordius hide the ends of the rope, that no one could see how to untie it.

After years of ruling wisely, Gordius died. But the knot

remained, and all strangers who came to the temple of Jupiter admired its design and strength.

"Only a very great man could have tied such a knot as that," said some.

"You have spoken truly," said the oracle of the temple. "But the man who undoes it will be much greater."

"What do you mean?" asked the visitors.

"The man who undoes this wonderful knot shall have the world for his kingdom," came the answer.

After that a great many people came every year to see the Gordian knot. Princes and warriors from every land tried to untie it. But the ends of the rope remained hidden, and they could not even make a beginning of the task.

Hundreds of years passed. King Gordius had been dead for so long that people remembered him only as the man who tied the wonderful knot, the knot that could not be undone.

Then there came into Phrygia a young king from Macedonia, far across the sea. The name of this young king was Alexander. He had conquered all of Greece, and now he had set his sights on Asia.

"Where is the fabled Gordian knot?" he asked.

The people led him into the temple of Jupiter and showed him the knot where Gordius had left it.

"What is it the oracle said about this knot?" Alexander asked.

"It said that the man who undoes it will have the world for his kingdom. But many have tried, and all have failed."

Alexander looked at the knot carefully. He could not find the ends, but what did that matter? He raised his sword and, with one stroke, cut it into so many pieces that the rope dropped to the ground.

"It is thus," said the young king, "that I cut all Gordian knots."

And then he went on with his little army to conquer Asia.

"The world is my kingdom," he said.

Grumble Town

FOLKTALE

There is nothing more unattractive than the sound of whining in the midst of plenty. It is not a good sign of character at any level—in individuals, families, communities, or nations as a whole.

There was once a place called Grumble Town where everybody grumbled, grumbled, grumbled. In summer, the people grumbled that it was too hot. In winter, it was too cold. When it rained, the children whimpered because they couldn't go outside. When the sun came out, they complained that they had nothing to do. Neighbors griped and groaned about neighbors, parents about children, brothers about sisters. Everybody had a problem, and everyone whined that *someone* should come do something about it. One day a peddler trudged into town, carrying a big basket on his back. When he heard all the fussing and sighing and moaning, he put his basket down and cried: "O citizens of this town! Your fields are ripe with grain, your orchards heavy with fruit. Your mountains are covered by good, thick forests, and your valleys watered by deep, wide rivers. Never have I seen a place blessed by such opportunity and abundance. Why are you so dissatisfied? Gather around me, and I will show you the way to contentment."

Now this peddler's shirt was tattered and torn. His pants showed patches, his shoes had holes. The people laughed to think that someone like him could show them how to be content. But while they snickered, he pulled a long rope from his basket and strung it between two poles in the town square. Then, holding his basket before him, he cried: "People of Grumble Town! Whoever is dissatisfied, write your trouble on a piece of paper, and bring it and put it in this basket. I will exchange your problem for happiness!"

The crowd swarmed around him. No one hesitated at the chance to get rid of his trouble. Every man, woman, and child in the village scribbled a grumble onto a scrap of paper and dropped it into the basket.

They watched as the peddler took each trouble and hung it on the line. By the time he was through, troubles fluttered on every inch of rope, from end to end. Then he said: "Now each one of you should take from this magic line the smallest trouble you can find."

They all rushed forward to examine all the troubles. They hunted and fingered and pondered, each trying to pick the very smallest trouble. After a while the magic line was empty.

And behold! Each held in his hand the very same trouble he had put into the basket. Each had chosen his own trouble, thinking it was the smallest of all on the line.

From that day, the people of Grumble Town stopped grumbling all the time. And whenever anyone had the urge to whimper or whine, he thought of the peddler and his magic line.

How They Built the Walls

RETOLD BY HENRY HALLAM TWEEDY

Any people who would build or preserve a nation should remember the courage, perseverance, vigilance, hard work, and faith of Nehemiah. Here are some of the virtues needed to make a country safe and strong. The story is from the book of Nehemiah in the Bible.

About 450 years before Jesus was born, there lived in the palace of the king of Persia a young Jew, whose name was Nehemiah. He seemed to have everything to make him happy. He had clothes of silk, and plenty of food, and could enjoy the fine things in the palace. Moreover, the king loved him and trusted him, so much so that he made Nehemiah his cupbearer. This meant a great deal in those days. For when wicked men wished to kill the king they used to try to put poison in his cup. Only a true friend might fill and bring it, and he would taste it before he gave it to the king to show that the king need not be afraid.

But with all this Nehemiah was not happy. For he was far

from the city where his fathers had lived and now were buried. He had friends there, whom he longed to see, and he was eager to make his home in the land of his people, and to serve it, and make it beautiful, and protect it against its foes.

One day his brother came to him with some men from Jerusalem, who brought bad news. They told him that his friends were poor, and that they were having a great deal of sorrow and trouble. As for the city, which he loved, its great wall, built to guard it from its enemies, was broken down, while the great gates, through which people might enter by day but which were closed to keep out foes and robbers at night, had been burned.

When Nehemiah heard this, he was very sad. He knew that wild animals could creep in and prowl around its streets at night. Worse yet, wild men could steal in under the cover of darkness, and rob his friends, and even kill them. Perhaps some cruel king would march against it with his soldiers, and burn all the homes and make the people his slaves. No wonder that Nehemiah was unhappy. He felt so bad that he sat down and cried, and for days and days he could not even bear to eat.

But there was no use in crying. He knew that. And to go without food would only make him weak and unable to work, while it would not build the walls of his city or bring aid to his friends. So he made up his mind to do something, and the first thing that he did was to ask God to help him and to guide him, so that he might go back home and serve his city and his friends. Then he arose, and made himself ready to act as cupbearer, and went in to wait on the king.

The king saw at once that his cupbearer's heart was full of sorrow. "Why are you sad," he asked, "inasmuch as you are not sick?"

At first Nehemiah was almost afraid to tell him, for while he knew that his city needed him, he feared that the king would not let him go. But at last he plucked up courage, and with a prayer in his heart that God would cause the king to be gracious, he made answer. "Why should I not be sad," he said, "when the city where my fathers are buried lies waste, and its walls are broken down, and its gates are burned?"

Then the king was sorry for him, and said, "What can I do for you? Come, tell me!"

Nehemiah bowed himself before the king, and said, "If I have pleased you and you really love me, send me to Jerusalem, that I may build its walls."

To his great joy, the king said that he might go. He even sent soldiers with him to guard him and help him. He also gave Nehemiah letters to his servants, who ruled for him in the land lying between Persia and Judah, bidding these men to give him wood with which to make the gates. So Nehemiah started out on his long journey, and at last found himself safe in Jerusalem among his friends.

It seemed wise not to tell them why he had come until he knew just what needed to be done. So one night Nehemiah and a few of his men walked around the city and looked at the walls. He soon saw that these were badly broken and quite useless, as the men had told him. Before the people were awake, he and his friends were back in their homes.

The next morning, he called the people together and said, "Come, and let us build the walls of our city! The king, my master, says that we may do so. God will help us, and if we love Him and obey Him, He will give us strength to drive away our foes."

Now, the wall was a very, very long one, and it had to be very
thick and very high. It seemed as if they never would be able to
finish it, and they could not have done so if they had not all
worked, and worked hard. There were doubtless some lazy men,
who did not want to work, and some cowards who were afraid
that foes would come and hurt them while they were at work,
and some greedy, selfish men, who did not love their city very
much, and said that unless Nehemiah paid them money they
would not work. But Nehemiah made the lazy men ashamed of
themselves, and cheered those who were afraid, and told the
selfish ones that if they did not work, their foes and robbers
would come and take away the money that they had already.

Most of the people worked with a will gladly, and began at
once to build next to their own homes. Some said that they
would build one gate, and some another. Both men and women
worked on the walls. The boys and girls were busy, too.
Everybody worked and sang and pounded and shouted as the
great stones were put into place. It was very hard labor. Their
hands were bruised and torn, and their arms ached, and their
backs were weary. But they loved their city dearly, and when
people work for somebody or something that they love, the
hardest toil is done gladly and often seems light.

Round about the country were men who hated Nehemiah
and his people. They did not want to have the walls built, for
then it would be harder to take the city, and they could not
break into it and make the people slaves. Some of them used to
stand near the men while they were at work, and laugh at them.
"You can never build such great walls," they cried. "What is the
use of trying!" When the people kept right on, they sent word,

saying that if the work was not stopped, they would come and fight. But Nehemiah told the people not to be afraid. "Trust God," he said, "and work with your trowel in one hand and your sword in the other."

Every day saw fewer holes in the walls of the city. One by one the big gates were made and swung into place. At last the great work was done, and Nehemiah and his friends were as happy as they were weary. No robbers could creep into their homes now. There would be no more wild beasts prowling around their streets at night. As for the men who had jeered at them and tried to stop the work, the workers could laugh at them now. The people had loved their city enough to labor for it, and to suffer hardship, and endure danger. But as the result of their work, it was now a strong fort, and their lives and their homes were safe once more. And the men and women and boys and girls who had helped Nehemiah were happy and loved the city better and were prouder of it because each had worked and done a full share in building the great wall.

Nehemiah did many other things to make his city better and more beautiful, and all men loved him and honored him, because he had served his country so well.

The Keys of Calais

ADAPTED FROM A RETELLING
BY CHARLOTTE YONGE

This story reminds us that those of high rank and achievement sometimes step forward to make the greatest sacrifices. Here are some noblemen who truly acted nobly.

In 1346, at the outset of the Hundred Years' War, King Edward III of England marched upon Calais, the most important town in northern France. He arrived before the town in early August, his good knights and squires arrayed in flashing armor, his stout archers wielding their deadly long-bows, his royal standards floating in the breeze above the whole glittering army. The walls of the city were of a huge thickness, with towers raised to a great height, and the king knew it would be useless to attempt a direct assault.

A herald, in a rich, long robe embroidered with the arms of England, rode up to the gate, a trumpet sounding before him, and called upon Sir Jean de Vienne, the governor of Calais, to surrender the place to Edward. Sir Jean made answer that he held the town for Philip, King of France, and that he would defend it to the last. The herald rode back again, and the English began the siege of the city. At first they covered the whole plain with their white canvas tents. Then, as time passed, they erected a little wooden town, with streets and a market and even a wooden palace for the king's comfort.

After a while a large and colorful fleet came crossing the waters from the white cliffs of Dover. King Edward and his knights rode down to the landing place to welcome the fair-haired Queen Philippa, and all her train of ladies. They had come from England in great numbers to visit their husbands, fathers, and brothers in their camp. Then there was a great court, and numerous feasts and dances, and the knights and squires were constantly striving to see who could do the bravest deed to please the ladies.

While this high merriment was going on outside their walls, the people of Calais were growing lean in the cheeks. At first a few brave French sailors, who knew the coast thoroughly, managed to guide little fleets of boats loaded with bread and meat into the city. They were often chased by Edward's vessels, and sometimes nearly taken, but they always managed to escape. So at last Edward, growing wrathful, built a great wooden castle on the seashore and filled it with archers and machines that tossed huge, ship-crushing stones. They kept such a watch upon the harbor that the French sailors dared not enter it. Then the townspeople began to feel what hunger really was.

One night the forlorn citizens looked down from their high walls and spied the thing they had been desperately awaiting—a great and noble French army spreading across the hillsides! It was a beautiful sight to the starving garrison to watch their countrymen pitching their white tents right behind the English forces, the knights' armor glancing and banners flying in the moonlight. King Philip had arrived to drive the invaders away!

But soon their hopes were dashed. King Philip was not eager to risk a defeat at the hands of the English. There were a few skirmishes. The armies traded insults and challenges. Three days of parleys ensued. Then, without the slightest real effort to rescue the brave, patient townspeople, away went King Philip of France with all his men. The people of Calais saw the French host that had crowded the hillside melt away like a summer cloud.

August had come again, and they had suffered privation for a whole year for the sake of a king who deserted them at their utmost need. They were in so grievous a state of hunger and distress that the hardiest could endure no more. The governor, Sir Jean de Vienne, went to the battlements and made signs he wished to hold a parley. He owned that the garrison was reduced to the greatest extremity of distress, and requested King Edward to be content with obtaining the city and its fortress, leaving the citizens and soldiers to depart in peace.

But Edward was so enraged at the delay and expense the siege had cost him, he would consent to receive the town only on unconditional terms. He would slay, or ransom, or make prisoner whomever he pleased, and he let it be known that there was a heavy reckoning to pay.

The town's brave answer was: "These conditions are too heavy for us. We are but a small number of knights and squires, who have loyally served our king, as you would have done. We have suffered greatly, but we will endure far more before we consent to endanger the children of our town. We therefore entreat you to reconsider."

The king was in a stern mood, and he answered that he would pardon the townspeople only on one condition. Six of the chief citizens of Calais must come forward with halters around their necks, carrying the keys to the town. These six the king would punish as he saw fit. The remainder of the inhabitants could go free.

On hearing this, Sir Jean de Vienne begged that he be allowed to consult the citizens. He went to the marketplace and rang a great bell, upon which all the townspeople assembled. As he told them the hard terms, he could not keep them from weeping bitterly. Should all starve together, or should they sacrifice their most honored comrades?

Then a voice was heard. It was that of the richest citizen in the town, Eustache de St. Pierre.

"Ladies and gentlemen, high and low," he said, "it would be a pity to cause so many people to die through hunger, if it could be prevented. To hinder it would be meritorious in the eyes of our Savior. I have such faith and trust in finding grace before God, if I die to save my townspeople, that I name myself of the first of the six."

As he ceased, his fellow townspeople wept aloud.

Another citizen, very rich and respected, rose and said: "I will be the second to my comrade Eustache," His name was Jean Daire. After Jacques Wistant, another very rich man, offered himself as a companion to these, who were both his cousins. His brother Pierre would not be left behind. Two others then named themselves to the gallant band, and the number demanded by Edward was complete.

The gates were opened, the governor and the six passed through, and the gates were again shut behind them. Sir Jean then rode out to the English representatives and told them how these six burghers had offered themselves up, and begged them to do all in their power to save them. The governor then went back to the town, full of grief.

The six citizens were led to the presence of the king in his full court. They all knelt down, and the foremost said: "Most gallant king, you see before you six citizens of Calais, who have been important merchants, and who bring to you the keys of the castle and the town. We yield ourselves to your absolute will and pleasure, in order to save the remainder of the inhabitants of Calais, who have suffered much distress and misery. Condescend, therefore, out of your nobleness of mind, to have mercy on us."

Pity stirred among all the English barons, knights, and squires assembled there. They saw the resigned faces, pale and thin with patiently endured hunger, of those venerable men, offering themselves in the cause of their fellow townspeople. They wept at the sight. But the king was unmoved. He cast angry glances at the six, and ordered their heads struck off.

The English knights begged the king to be more merciful. They told him that such an execution would tarnish his honor. They warned that reprisals would be made against his own garrisons. They pointed to the selflessness and nobility of the six. But the king would not listen. He sent for the headsman and his great ax.

Then suddenly the queen of England, her eyes streaming

with tears, threw herself on her knees among the captives and cried; "Ah, gentle sir, I have crossed the sea, with so much danger, to be with you. I have never asked you one favor. But now I ask as a gift, for the sake of the Son of the Blessed Mary, and for your love to me, that you will spare these six men!"

For some time the king looked at her in silence. Then he exclaimed, "Dame, dame, I wish you had been anywhere else but here! You have entreated in such a manner that I cannot refuse you. I therefore give you these men, to do as you please with them."

The queen conducted the six citizens to her own chambers, where she made them welcome and had the halters taken from their necks. She clothed them, and fed them, and gave them gifts to remember her by. Then she saw them safely escorted out of the English camp. Such is the story of six brave and patient men who went forth, by their own free will, to meet what might have been a cruel death, in order to obtain the safety of their fellow townspeople.

King Alfred and the Cakes

ADAPTED FROM JAMES BALDWIN

Alfred the Great was king of the West Saxons in England during the ninth century. His determination to protect England from Danish conquest and his emphasis on literacy and education for his people have lifted him into the ranks of England's most popular rulers. This famous story reminds us that attention to little duties prepares us to meet larger ones. It also reminds us that leadership and responsibility walk hand in hand and that truly great leaders do not disdain small responsibilities.

In England many years ago there ruled a king named Alfred. A wise and just man, Alfred was one of the best kings England ever had. Even today, centuries later, he is known as Alfred the Great.

The days of Alfred's rule were not easy ones in England. The country was invaded by the fierce Danes, who had come from across the sea. There were so many Danish invaders, and they were so strong and bold, that for a long time they won almost every battle. If they kept on winning, they would soon be masters of the whole country.

At last, after so many struggles, King Alfred's English army was broken and scattered. Every man had to save himself in the best way he could, including King Alfred. He disguised himself as a shepherd and fled alone through the woods and swamps.

After several days of wandering, he came to the hut of a woodcutter. Tired and hungry, he knocked on the door and begged the woodcutter's wife to give him something to eat and a place to sleep.

The woman looked with pity at the ragged fellow. She had no idea who he really was. "Come in," she said. "I will give you some supper if you will watch these cakes I am baking on the hearth. I want to go out and milk the cow. Watch them carefully, and make sure they don't burn while I'm gone."

Alfred thanked her politely and sat down beside the fire. He tried to pay attention to the cakes, but soon all his troubles filled his mind. How was he going to get his army together again? And even if he did, how was he going to prepare it to face the Danes? How could he possibly drive such fierce invaders out of England? The more he thought, the more hopeless the future seemed, and he began to believe there was no use in continuing to fight. Alfred saw only his problems. He forgot he was in the woodcutter's hut, he forgot about his hunger, and he forgot all about the cakes.

In a little while, the woman came back. She found her hut full of smoke and her cakes burned to a crisp. And there was Alfred sitting beside the hearth, gazing into the flames. He had never even noticed the cakes were burning.

"You lazy, good-for-nothing fellow!" the woman cried. "Look what you've done! You want something to eat, but you don't want to work for it! Now none of us will have any supper!" Alfred only hung his head in shame.

Just then the woodcutter came home. As soon as he walked through the door, he recognized the stranger sitting at his hearth.

King John and the Magna Carta

RETOLD BY JAMES BALDWIN

Here is a leader of the church doing his part to establish the rights of Englishmen, which in time would come to mean human rights. More than once in the course of Western civilization has the courage of religious leaders become the seed of political achievement. The Magna Carta was signed in 1215.

King John was so selfish and cruel that all the people in his kingdom both feared and hated him.

One by one he lost the dominions in France which the former kings of England had held. Men called him Lackland, because in the end he had neither lands nor castles that he could rightfully call his own.

He robbed his people. He quarreled with his knights and barons. He offended all good men. He formed a plan for making war against King Philip of France, and called upon his barons to join him. When some of them refused, he burned their castles and destroyed their fields.

At last the barons met together at a place called Saint Edmundsbury to talk about their grievances. "Why should we submit to be ruled by such a king?" said some of the boldest. But most of them were afraid to speak their minds.

Stephen Langton, the Archbishop of Canterbury, was with them, and there was no bolder friend of liberty than he. He made a stirring speech that gave courage even to the most cowardly.

"Are you men?" he said. "Why then do you submit to this false-hearted king? Stand up and declare your freedom. Refuse to be the slaves of this man. Demand the rights and privileges that belong to you as free men. Put this demand in writing—in the form of a great charter—and require the king to sign it. So shall it be to you and your children a safeguard forever against the injustice of unworthy rulers."

The barons were astonished at the boldness of this speech. Some of them shrank back in fear, but the bravest among them showed by their looks and gestures that they were ready to make a bold stand for liberty.

"Come forward!" cried Stephen Langton. "Come, and swear that you will never rest until King John has given you the rights that are yours. Swear that you will have the charter from his hand, or that you will wage war upon him to the very death."

Never before had Englishmen heard such a speech. The barons took the oath which Stephen Langton prescribed. Then they gathered their fighting men together and marched upon London. The cowardly king was frightened.

"What do these men want?" he asked.

They sent him word that they wanted their rights as Englishmen, and that they would never rest until he had given them a charter of liberties signed by his own hand.

"Oh, well! If that is all, you shall surely have it," he said.

But he put them off with one excuse and another. He sent a messenger to Rome to ask the Pope to help him. He tried, by fine promises, to persuade Stephen Langton to abandon the cause he had undertaken. But no one knew the falseness of his heart better than the Pope and the Archbishop of Canterbury.

The people from all parts of the country now came and joined the army of the barons. Of all the knights in England, only seven remained true to the king.

The barons made out a list of their demands, and Stephen Langton carried it to the king. "These things we will have," they said, "and there shall be no peace until you grant them."

Oh, how angry was King John! He raved like a wild beast; he clenched his fists; he stamped upon the floor. But he saw that he was helpless. At last he said that he would sign the charter at such time and place as the barons might name.

"Let the time be the fifteenth of June," they said, "and let the place be Runnymede."

Now, Runnymede was a green meadow not far from the city of London, and there the king went with his few followers. He was met by the barons, with an army of determined men behind them.

The charter which Stephen Langton and his friends had drawn up was spread out before the king. He was not a scholar, and so it was read to him, line by line. It was a promise that the people should not be oppressed; that the rights of the cities and boroughs should be respected; that no man should be imprisoned without a fair trial; that justice should not be delayed or denied to anyone.

Pale with anger, the king signed the charter, and then rode back to his castle at Windsor. As soon as he was in his own chamber he began to rave like a madman. He rolled on the floor. He beat the air with his fists. He gnawed sticks and straws. He foamed at the mouth. He cursed the barons and the people for treating their king so badly.

But he was helpless. The charter was signed—the Magna Carta, to which Englishmen still point as the first safeguard of their rights and liberties.

As might have been expected, it was not long before John tried to break all his promises. The barons made war upon him, and never again did he see a peaceful day. His anger and anxiety caused him to fall into a fever which nothing could cure. At last, despised and shunned as he deserved to be, he died. I doubt if there was an eye in England that wept for him.

The Lady with the Lamp

ELMER ADAMS AND WARREN FOSTER

Born in 1820 to wealthy parents, Florence Nightingale spent her childhood on comfortable family estates in England. When she was sixteen years old, she thought she heard the voice of God informing her that she had a specific mission in life. For the next few years she spent more and more of her time studying public health and reforms to aid the suffering. In 1850, against her family's wishes, she attended a training school for nurses, and at age thirty-three she became superintendent of a women's hospital in London.

In 1854, when England and France went to war with Russia in the Crimea, the British people grew outraged over reports of sick and wounded soldiers dying in disgraceful conditions. At the appeal of the minister of war, Nightingale traveled to Scutari, Turkey, to take charge of the military hospital there. She stepped ashore to discover scores of maimed troops just arrived from the Battle of Balaklava, where the disastrous Charge of the Light Brigade had occurred. The story of how this heroine rescued Scutari and founded the modern nursing profession is the stuff of legend. It was not only Florence Nightingale's remarkable organizational and administrative skills that saved the day. It was the

*force of her remarkable character—her compassion, her courage, her
perseverance.*

The Crimean War was in progress, France and England
being allied to defend Turkey against Russian aggression.
The British army had sailed to a strange climate with shame-
fully poor commissary and medical staffs. The weather was
stormy and the soldiers had little shelter against it. Said a correspondent of the *London Times,* "It is now pouring rain, the
skies are black as ink, the wind is howling over the staggering
tents, the trenches are turned into dikes; in the tents the water
is sometimes a foot deep; our men have not either warm or
waterproof clothing; they are out for twelve hours at a time in
the trenches"—and so on without end.

Plenty of food and clothing had been shipped from England,
but they never reached their destination. Some vessels were
delayed; in some the stores were packed at the bottom of the
hold and could not be raised; some hove in with the wrong
goods at the wrong port—and, on one, the consignment of
boots proved to be all for the left foot! But the most criminal
point of mismanagement was this: Food, clothing, and medicine might be stored in a warehouse within easy reach of the
army, but the official with authority to deal them out would be
absent, and so stringent were the army rules that no one dared
so much as point at them! The rigid system was infinitely worse
than no system. And the soldiers were starving in the midst of
plenty, and freezing under the shadow of mountains of good
woolen clothing.

Now, to come at once to the worst, imagine these conditions transferred to the military hospitals. In the great Barrack Hospital at Scutari lay two thousand sorely wounded men, and hundreds more were coming in every day. The wards were crowded to twice their capacity—the sick lay side by side on mattresses that touched each other. The floors and walls and ceilings were wet and filthy. There was no ventilation. Rats and vermin swarmed everywhere. The men lay "in their uniforms, stiff with gore and covered with filth to a degree and of a kind no one could write about." It was a "dreadful den of dirt, pestilence, and death."

It is difficult to imagine a scene of worse disorder and misery. The proportion of deaths to the whole army, from disease alone—malaria and cholera—was sixty percent. Seventy died in the hospital in one night. There was danger that the entire army would be wiped out—most of it without ever receiving a scratch from the enemy's weapons.

It was in this extremity that the British nation appealed to Florence Nightingale to save the sick and wounded men—an army of twenty-eight thousand as helpless as children before the ravages of disease—and to save the war. The minister of war requested her to organize a band of nurses for Scutari and gave her power to draw upon the government to any extent.

Miss Nightingale at the time was thirty-four years old. An acquaintance described her thus: "Simple, intellectual, sweet, full of love and benevolence, she is a fascinating and perfect woman. She is tall and pale. Her face is exceedingly lovely. But better than all is the soul's glory that shines through every feature so exultingly. Nothing can be sweeter than her smile. It is like a sunny day in summer."

Within six days from the time she accepted the post, Miss Nightingale had selected thirty-eight nurses, and departed for the seat of war. She arrived at Scutari November 4, 1854, and walked the length of the barracks, viewing her two miles of patients. And next day before she could form any plans, the fresh victims of another battle began to arrive. There was not space for them within the walls and hundreds had to repose, with what comfort they could, in the mud outside. One of the nurses wrote, "Many died immediately after being brought in—their moans would pierce the heart—and the look of agony on those poor dying faces will never leave my heart."

But the nurse did not hesitate. She ordered the patients brought in, and directed where to lay them, and what attention they should have. She was up and around twenty hours that day, and as many the next, until a place had been found for every man, even in the corridors and on the landings of the stairs. As leader of the nurses she might have confined herself to administrative tasks—of which there were enough for any woman—and stayed in the office. But no. She shrank from the sight of no operation. Many men, indeed, whose cases the surgeons thought hopeless, she nursed back to health. A visitor saw her one morning at two o'clock at the bedside of a dying soldier, lamp in hand. She was writing down his last message to the home folks; and for them, too, she took in charge his watch and trinkets—and then soothed him in his last moments. And this was but one case in thousands. "She is a ministering angel, without any exaggeration, in these hospitals," wrote a correspondent of the *London Times,* "and as the slender form glides quietly along each corridor, every poor fellow's face softens with gratitude at the sight of her. When all the medical officers have retired for the night, and silence and darkness have settled down upon the miles of prostrate sick, she may be observed alone, with lamp in hand, making her solitary rounds."

In a place like Scutari, however, this kind of feminine tenderness alone would avail little. Science was needed, the most perfect skill in scientific nursing. The windows were few, and the few were mostly locked; and where one was opened the odors of decaying animals came in to pollute still more the foul air of the wards.

The food for the whole hospital—for those sick of fever, cholera, wounds, and what not, as well as for those in health—was cooked, like an "Irish stew," in big kettles. Vegetables and meats were dumped in together, and when anyone felt hungry he could dip for himself. Naturally some got food overdone, and some got it raw; the luckiest got a mess that was scarcely palatable; and the sick could generally not eat at all. As for other matters, it has been shown how unclean the barrack wards were, how "only seven shirts" had been laundered in all those wretched weeks, and how the infected bed linen of all classes of patients was thrown, unsorted, into one general wash.

But Florence Nightingale had spent twelve years in the hospitals of Europe to learn how to conquer just such situations as this. She had the waste and pollution outside the walls cleared away. Then she threw up the windows, and set a carpenter to make more. Within ten days she had established a diet kitchen and was feeding the men each on the food his particular case demanded. She set up a laundry, too, where the garments of the sick could be cleansed in a sanitary way. All this was the easier to do because with wise foresight she had brought the necessary articles with her on the *Victus* from England. The ship gave up chicken, jelly, and all manner of delicacies; and, on a single day, "a thousand shirts, besides other clothing." In two weeks that "dreadful den of dirt, pestilence, and death" had vanished; and in its place stood a building, light and well aired throughout, where patients lay on spotless cots, ate appetizing food from clean dishes, had their baths and their medicine at regular intervals, and never for an hour lacked any attention that would help their recovery.

But after all is said of Florence Nightingale's sympathy and her science, she owed her final triumph in the Crimea to a rarer talent, that of tactful organizing and executive power. Why was she not tethered by the system and the red tape that rendered ineffectual the best efforts of the medical men? Most things needful were in store not far from the barracks hospital. But the regular physicians could not get at them. Why could she?

In the first place she had tact enough not to offend the system. The minister of war had warned her, "A number of sentimental, enthusiastic ladies turned loose into the hospital at Scutari would probably after a few days be *'mises aag la porte'* by those whose business they would interrupt and whose authority they would dispute." Florence Nightingale did not at first interrupt or dispute anybody. She began by doing the neglected minor things, the things that no one else had time for. She opened windows. She scrubbed floors and walls. She laundered shirts. She peeled potatoes and boiled soup. She bathed the patients, dosed them with medicine while the worn-out surgeons were asleep, read to them, and wrote letters for them. In these activities she asked not even supplies from the system, but procured them from her own ship.

The hidebound officials were even then slow to concur. Perhaps they were jealous to see their own incompetence exposed. And there was one case—just one—where she came to blows with them. The hospital inmates were in desperate want, and the articles for their relief were nearby in a warehouse, but the stores could not be disturbed until after inspection. Miss Nightingale tried to hasten the inspection. Failing of that, she tried to get them distributed without inspection. That also failed. "My soldiers are dying," she said. "I must have those stores." Whereupon, she called two soldiers, marched them to the warehouse, and bade them burst open the doors!

That was the kind of firm hand she could use. More often, though, she attained her ends in a peaceful way. Only a little feminine tact was necessary to bring together the dilatory members of a board and get them to unlock a storehouse. She was soon able to lay her hands on an abundance of anything the situation demanded. Then, besides her own small band of nurses, a large number of orderlies and common soldiers were, after a time, detailed to work under her direction. "Never," she says, "came from them one word or one look which a gentleman would not have used"; and many of them became attached to her with an almost slavish affection.

And the result of her efforts justified this faith. When she arrived the death rate was sixty percent. She reduced it in a few weeks to one percent. Nine of her nurses died on duty; others were invalided home; she herself was long fever sick and near to death. But for two years she battled against disease, always in a winning fight. She conquered disease. And it is not too much to say that she conquered the Russian army, and saved the war for the allies. No wonder England welcomed her home as one of the greatest heroines in all its history.

The Maid of Orleans

ADAPTED FROM
LOUIS MAURICE BOUTET DE MONVEL

Here is one of the most famous heroines of all time, a sweet peasant girl who challenged kings, led her troops, and died for love of God and country.

She was born Joan d'Arc in 1412, in the little French village of Domremy. Her parents were honest laboring folk who lived by their toil. Their little house stood so close to the church that its garden touched the graveyard.

The child grew up there, under the eye of God.

She was a sweet, upright girl. Everyone loved her, for all knew her kind heart. A brave worker, she aided her family in their labors. By day she led the beasts to pasture, and in the evening she sat spinning by her mother's side.

She loved God, and often prayed to Him.

Now, in those days, France and England were at war. France had no real ruler. The English king had invaded the land, determined to make it his own. The French did not want to be ruled by the English, and they fought to put Charles the Dauphin, the son of their last king, on the throne.

But the dauphin had no army, no money, and no will to fight. Day by day, pieces of his kingdom fell away to the enemy. Famine and anarchy reigned across the land.

One summer day, when she was thirteen years old, Joan heard a voice at midday in her father's garden. It told her to be a good girl and go to church. Then it told her that she was to save all of France, and that she must go to help the dauphin.

"But I am only a poor girl," cried Joan.

"God will help thee," answered the voice.

And the child, overcome, was left weeping.

From that day she began to spend more and more time away from her playmates, listening to heavenly voices. As time passed, they became more urgent. The peril was great, they said; she must go help the king and save the kingdom.

And, of course, when Joan began to speak of her mission, many people laughed, and called her crazy. But the simple-hearted folk, moved by her faith, believed in her. A kind squire offered to take her to see the dauphin. The poor folk, adding their mites together, raised the money to clothe and arm the little peasant girl. They bought her a horse, and on the appointed day she set out with a small escort.

"God keep you!" cried the multitude, and they wept.

The enemy held the country through which the little party was to pass. They had to travel at night and hide through the day. Joan's companions, alarmed, spoke of turning back.

"Fear nothing," said she. "God is leading us."

On the twelfth day they arrived at the court of the dauphin. At first it looked as if he would not receive the inspired girl. But at last an interview was granted. One evening, by the light of fifty torches, Joan was brought into the great hall of the castle, crowded with all the nobles of the court. She had never seen the dauphin.

To see if God were really guiding her, as she claimed, the dauphin changed places with one of the noblemen in the court, and disguised himself in plain clothes. But Joan singled him out among the multitude at once, and knelt before him.

"God give you a happy life, gentle dauphin," she said.

"I am not the king," he answered. "Yonder is the king."

"You are he, gentle prince, and no other," she replied with perfect confidence. Then she told him that God had sent her to aid him, and asked for troops to save the city of Orleans, which lay under siege by the English troops. Everyone knew that if Orleans fell, France would be lost.

The king hesitated. The girl might be a sorceress. He sent her to be examined by learned men. For three weeks they tormented her with their questions. When they told her that God should have no need of men-at-arms to deliver France, she drew herself up quickly. "The soldiers will fight, but God will give the victory," she said.

The people declared that the maid was indeed inspired, and the learned and powerful were forced to yield to the multitude.

The French troops assembled. On Thursday, the 28th of April, 1429, the little army moved forward, led by Joan. She was clad in glistening armor, and carried a white banner embroidered with the lilies of France. When she entered Orleans, the people crowded to meet her. She passed by torchlight through the city; men, women, and children thronged to get near her, stretching forth their hands to touch the inspired maiden's horse.

Joan spoke kindly to them, promising to deliver the city. Her confidence influenced everyone around her. The people of Orleans, so lately timid and discouraged, now wished to hurl themselves at the enemy. Joan, meanwhile, had letters thrown over the walls of the city, ordering the besieging English to depart and return to their own country. They answered her with insults. So Joan mounted her war-horse and led her soldiers into battle.

Around Orleans stood the forts which the English held. The French now captured them one by one. Soon all but the last was taken from the enemy. Its walls were forbidding, and the French generals wanted to wait for more soldiers before making an attack. But Joan pushed them on.

The fighting was fierce. At one point Joan descended into a moat, and was raising a ladder against a parapet when an English arrow struck her between her neck and shoulder. She fell backward into the trench and, thinking her killed, the English rallied. But the brave girl pulled the arrow out of the wound, and was soon foremost in the fight again.

"Forward!" she cried. "All is yours!"

The English were routed. And Orleans, which had been besieged for eight months, was delivered in only four days.

The Maid of Orleans, as she was now called, hastened to the court of the dauphin. She desired at once to take him to Rheims, where he could be crowned. He received her with great honors, but refused to follow her. He accepted the devotion of the heroic girl, but did not want her generous efforts to disturb his easy life. Instead, he sent her to attack the places still held by the English on the banks of the river Loire.

In battle after battle, the French were victorious. Joan was always in the front of the ranks. She constantly exposed herself to blows and was often wounded, but would never use her sword. Her only weapon was her banner painted with the lilies of France.

At last the dauphin agreed to proceed to Rheims. On the 16th of July he entered the town at the head of his troops. The next day in the cathedral, with Joan standing at his side, he was crowned Charles VII of France.

But after the coronation, Joan seemed to lose her power. She began to lose battles. While defending the town of Compiègne, her army was driven back. During the retreat, Joan, deserted by all, found herself nearly surrounded by the enemy. She parried the blows of her assailants, steadily retreating until she reached the walls of the city. A step more and she would have been safe inside; but through either jealousy, imprudence, or treason, those who were defending the entrance to the city closed the gates and raised the bridge, leaving Joan outside. She fell into the hands of the English.

Ashamed at having been beaten so many times by a mere girl, her captors accused her of sorcery. They dragged her from prison to prison, and finally shut her up in a dungeon at Rouen. They brought her out for examination as many as sixteen times, worried her with all sorts of perplexing questions, then shut her up again. They used torture to make her confess that heaven had not sent her.

Many of the English believed that while Joan lived they

would be defeated, so they clamored for her death. A tribunal composed of bribed French priests was given the power to try her as a witch and a heretic. The unhappy maiden could oppose the insidious questions of her judges only with the uprightness and simplicity of her heart. "I have nothing more to do here," she said. "Send me back to God, from Whom I came." After a long trial and painful imprisonment, Joan was condemned and sentenced to be burned at the stake.

And throughout her ordeal, King Charles of France, who owed her so much, made no attempt to help her.

On the morning of May 30, 1431, at nine o'clock, Joan rode through the streets of Rouen in the executioner's cart. On seeing the pile placed in front of the old marketplace, a cry escaped her.

"Ah, Rouen, Rouen, are you then to be my last home?" she exclaimed.

She knelt and prayed. Then, turning to her judges and enemies, she begged them to have a Mass said for her soul. She mounted the pile, and while they bound her hands, she asked to be shown a crucifix. Then they lit the fire. In the midst of the clouds of smoke and lurid gleam of flames, she forgave all, and said her last prayer.

Everyone present wept, even the executioners and judges. It is said that many turned away, unable to bear the sight, and as they fled cried: "We are lost! We have burned a saint!"

Man Enough for the Job

Retold by Ella Lyman Cabot

Great men do not disdain small duties.

An incident is told of the first American war, about an officer who set his men to fell some trees which were needed to make a bridge. There were not nearly enough men, and work was getting on very slowly. Up rode a commanding-looking man and spoke to the officer in charge, who was urging on his men but doing nothing himself. "You haven't enough men for the job, have you?"

"No, sir. We need some help."

"Why don't you lend a hand yourself?" asked the man on horseback.

"Me, sir? Why, I am a corporal," replied the officer, looking rather affronted at the suggestion.

"Ah, true," quietly replied the other, and getting off his horse he labored with the men until the job was done. Then he mounted again, and as he rode off he said to the officer, "Corporal, the next time you have a job to put through and too few men to do it, you had better send for the commander in chief, and I will come again."

It was General Washington.

The Man Who Would Not Drink Alone

ADAPTED FROM A RETELLING
BY ROSALIE KAUFMAN

Loyalty is a two-way street; sharing hardship is the mark of a loyal leader. The ancient historian Plutarch recounts this tale about Alexander the Great (356–323 B.C.).

Alexander the Great was leading his army homeward after his great victory against Porus in India. The country through which they now marched was bare and desert, and his army suffered dreadfully from heat, hunger, and, most of all, thirst. The soldiers' lips cracked and their throats burned from want of water, and many were ready to lie down and give up.

About noon one day the army met a party of Greek travelers. They were on mules, and carried with them a few vessels filled with water. One of them, seeing the king almost choking from thirst, filled a helmet and offered it to him.

Alexander took it into his hands, then looked around at the faces of his suffering soldiers, who craved refreshment just as much as he did.

"Take it away," he said, "for if I drink alone, the rest will be out of heart, and you have not enough for all."

So he handed the water back without touching a drop of it. And the soldiers, cheering their king, leaped to their feet, and demanded to be led forward.

Margaret of New Orleans

SARA CONE BRYANT

Here is a true story of a real heroine. Born of Irish immigrant parents, Margaret Haughery moved to New Orleans from Baltimore in search of health for her husband. When both her husband and child died, she began helping the children of the Poydras Orphan Asylum. Most of the money she earned from her dairy and bakery went to the city's needy, and when Margaret died her life savings of $30,000 went to charity. The Margaret Statue, one of the earliest memorials erected to a woman in the United States, was dedicated in 1884. It still stands today, modest and compelling.

There is still work like this to be done in cities all over the country, and more Margarets needed to do it.

If you ever go to the beautiful city of New Orleans, somebody will be sure to take you down into the old business part of the city, where there are banks and shops and hotels, and show you a statue which stands in a little square there. It is the statue of a woman, sitting in a low chair, with her arms around a child, who leans against her. The woman is not at all pretty. She wears thick, common shoes, a plain dress, with a little shawl, and a sunbonnet. She is stout and short, and her face is a square-chinned Irish face. But her eyes look at you like your mother's.

Now there is something very surprising about this statue. It was one of the first that was ever made in this country in honor of a woman. Even in old Europe there are not many monuments to women, and most of the few are to great queens or princesses, very beautiful and very richly dressed. You see, this statue in New Orleans is not quite like anything else.

It is the statue of a woman named Margaret. Her whole name was Margaret Haughery, but no one in New Orleans remembers her by it, any more than you think of your dearest sister by her full name. She is just Margaret. This is her story, and it tells why people made a monument for her.

When Margaret was a tiny baby, her father and mother died, and she was adopted by two young people as poor and as kind as her own parents. She lived with them until she grew up. Then she married, and had a little baby of her own. But very soon her husband died, and then the baby died, too, and Margaret was all alone in the world. She was poor, but she was strong, and knew how to work.

All day, from morning until evening, she ironed clothes in a laundry. And every day, as she worked by the window, she saw the little motherless children from the orphanage nearby working and playing about. After a while, a great sickness came upon the city, and so many mothers and fathers died that there were more orphans than the orphanage could possibly take care of. They needed a good friend now. You would hardly think, would you, that a poor woman who worked in a laundry could be much of a friend to them? But Margaret was. She went straight to the kind Sisters who ran the orphanage and told them she was going to give them part of her wages and was going to work for them, besides. Pretty soon she had worked so hard that she had some money saved from her wages. With this, she bought two cows and a little delivery cart. Then she carried her milk to her customers in the little cart every morning, and as she went, she begged the leftover food from the hotels and rich houses, and brought it back in the cart to the hungry children in the orphanage. In the very hardest times that was often all the food the children had.

A part of the money Margaret earned went every week to the orphanage, and after a few years it was made very much larger and better. And Margaret was so careful and so good at business that, in spite of her giving, she bought more cows and earned more money. With this, she built a home for orphan babies; she called it her baby house.

After a time, Margaret had a chance to get a bakery, and then she became a bread-woman instead of a milk-woman. She carried the bread just as she had carried the milk, in her cart. And still she kept giving money to the orphanage. Then the great war came, the Civil War. In all the trouble and sickness and fear of that time, Margaret drove her cart of bread, and somehow she had always enough to give the starving soldiers, and for her babies, besides what she sold. And despite all this, she earned enough so that when the war was over she built a big steam factory for her bread. By this time everybody in the city knew her. The children all over the city loved her. The businessmen were proud of her. The poor people all came to her for advice. She used to sit at the open door of her office, in a calico gown and a little shawl, and give a good word to everybody, rich or poor.

Then, by and by, one day, Margaret died. And when it was time to read her will, the people found that, with all her giving, she had still saved a great deal of money, and that she had left every cent of it to the different orphanages of the city — each one of them was given something. Whether they were for white children or black, for Jews, Catholics, or Protestants, made no difference; for Margaret always said, "They are all orphans alike." And just think, that splendid, wise will was signed with a cross instead of a name, for Margaret had never learned to read or write!

When the people of New Orleans knew that Margaret was dead, they said, "She was a mother to the motherless. She was a friend to those who had no friends. She had wisdom greater than schools can teach. We will not let her memory go from us." So they made a statue of her, just as she used to look, sitting in her own office door, or driving in her own little cart. And there it stands today, in memory of the great love and the great power of plain Margaret Haughery, of New Orleans.

The Moses of Her People

SARAH BRADFORD

Harriet Tubman was born into slavery on a Maryland plantation around 1821. Like most slaves, she received no education and could not read or write. In 1844 her owner forced her to marry a fellow slave, John Tubman. One summer night in 1849, she began to walk north toward her freedom. She later returned to help members of her family escape, and eventually made some twenty trips into the South to guide three hundred slaves along the Underground Railroad to Northern havens. With the outbreak of the Civil War, she traveled to South Carolina with the Union army to serve as a nurse, cook, scout, and spy. After the war, she continued to work to improve freed slaves' conditions.

The following account is from the first biography of Harriet Tubman, published in 1869 and in revised form in 1886; it rightly calls her "the Moses of Her People."

One day there were scared faces seen in the Negro quarter, and hurried whispers passed from one to another. No one knew how it had come out, but someone had heard that

Harriet and two of her brothers were very soon, perhaps today, perhaps tomorrow, to be sent far south with a gang, bought up for plantation work. Harriet was about twenty or twenty-five years old at this time, and the constantly recurring idea of escape at *sometime,* took sudden form that day, and with her usual promptitude of action she was ready to start at once.

She held a hurried consultation with her brothers, in which she so wrought upon their fears that they expressed themselves as willing to start with her that very night, for that far North, where, could they reach it in safety, freedom awaited them.

The brothers started with her, but the way was strange, the North was far away, and all unknown, the masters would pursue and recapture them, and their fate would be worse than ever before. And so they broke away from her, and bidding her good-bye, they hastened back to the known horrors of slavery, and the dread of that which was worse.

Harriet was now left alone, but after watching the retreating forms of her brothers, she turned her face toward the north, and fixing her eyes on the guiding star, and committing her way unto the Lord, she started again upon her long, lonely journey. Her farewell song was long remembered in the cabins, and the old mother sat and wept for her lost child. No intimation had been given her of Harriet's intention, for the old woman was of a most impulsive disposition, and her cries and lamentations would have made known to all within hearing Harriet's intended escape. With only the North Star for her guide, our heroine started on the way to liberty.

And so without money, and without friends, she started on through unknown regions; walking by night, hiding by day, but always conscious of an invisible pillar of cloud by day, and of fire by night, under the guidance of which she journeyed or rested. Without knowing whom to trust, or how near the pursuers might be, she carefully felt her way, and by her native cunning, or by God-given wisdom, she managed to apply to the right people for food, and sometimes for shelter; though often her bed was only the cold ground, and her watchers the stars of night.

After many long and weary days of travel, she found that she had passed the magic line, which then divided the land of bondage from the land of freedom. But where were the lovely white ladies whom in her visions she had seen, who, with arms outstretched, welcomed her to their hearts and homes? All these visions proved deceitful: She was more alone than ever; but she had crossed the line; no one could take her now, and she would never call any man "Master" more. . . .

It would be impossible here to give a detailed account of the journeys and labors of this intrepid woman for the redemption of her kindred and friends during the years that followed. Those years were spent in work, almost by night and day, with the one object of the rescue of her people from slavery. All her wages were laid away with this sole purpose, and as soon as a sufficient amount was secured, she disappeared from her Northern home, and as suddenly and mysteriously she appeared some dark night at the door of one of the cabins on a plantation, where a trembling band of fugitives, forewarned as to time and place, were anxiously awaiting their deliverer. Then she piloted them north, traveling by night, hiding by day, scaling the mountains, fording the rivers, threading the forests, lying concealed as the pursuers passed them. She, carrying the babies, drugged with paregoric, in a basket on her arm. So she went *nineteen* times, and so she brought away over three hundred pieces of living and breathing "property," with God-given souls. . . .

On one of their journeys to the North, as she was piloting a company of refugees, Harriet came, just as morning broke, to a town where a colored man had lived whose house had been one of her stations of the underground, or unseen railroad. They reached the house, and leaving her party huddled together in the middle of the street, in a pouring rain, Harriet went to the door, and gave the peculiar rap which was her customary signal to her friends. There was not the usual ready response, and she was obliged to repeat the signal several times. At length a window was raised, and the head of a *white man* appeared, with the gruff question, "Who are you?" and "What do you want?" Harriet asked after her friend, and was told that he had been obliged to leave for "harboring niggers."

Here was an unforeseen trouble; day was breaking, and daylight was the enemy of the hunted and flying fugitives. Their faithful leader stood one moment in the street, and in that moment she had flashed a message quicker than that of the telegraph to her unseen Protector, and the answer came as quickly in a suggestion to her of an almost forgotten place of refuge. Outside of the town there was a little island in a swamp, where the grass grew tall and rank, and where no human being could be suspected of seeking a hiding place. To this spot she conducted her party; she waded the swamp, carrying in a basket two well-drugged babies (these were a pair of little twins, whom I have since seen well-grown young women), and the rest of the company following. She ordered them to lie down in the tall, wet grass, and here she prayed again, and waited for deliverance. The poor creatures were all cold, and wet, and hungry, and Harriet did not dare to leave them to get supplies. For no doubt the man at whose house she had knocked, had given the alarm in the town; and officers might be on the watch for them. They were truly in a wretched condition, but Harriet's faith never wavered, her silent prayer still ascended, and she confidently expected help from some quarter or other.

It was after dusk when a man came slowly walking along the solid pathway on the edge of the swamp. He was clad in the garb of a Quaker, and proved to be a "friend" in need and in deed. He seemed to be talking to himself, but ears quickened by sharp practice caught the words he was saying:

"My wagon stands in the barnyard of the next farm across the way. The horse is in the stable; the harness hangs on a nail." And the man was gone. Night fell, and Harriet stole forth to the place designated. Not only a wagon, but a wagon well provisioned stood in the yard; and before many minutes the party were rescued from their wretched position, and were on their way rejoicing to the next town. Here dwelt a Quaker whom Harriet knew, and he readily took charge of the horse and wagon, and no doubt returned them to their owner. How the good man who thus came to their rescue had received any intimation of their being in the neighborhood Harriet never knew. But these sudden deliverances never seemed to strike her as at all strange or mysterious; her prayer was the prayer of faith, and she *expected* an answer.

Mother Holly

RETOLD BY ETTA AUSTIN BLAISDELL AND
MARY FRANCES BLAISDELL

*The Brothers Grimm, who collected this story, tell us that in
Germany people say, "Mother Holly is making her bed" whenever it
snows. In this tale, idleness and industry get their just rewards when
helping Mother Holly with her chores becomes a test of character for
two sisters.*

A widow, who lived in a cottage at a little distance from the
village, had two daughters. One of them was beautiful and
industrious, the other idle and ugly.

The mother loved the ugly one best, because she was her
own child. She cared so little for the other that she made her do
all the work and be like a Cinderella in the house.

Poor maiden, she was obliged to go every day and seat herself beside a well which stood near the broad highway. Here she
had to sit and spin until she thought her poor, tired fingers
would fall off.

One day when the spindle was so covered with dust that she could not use it, she rose and dipped it in the water of the well to wash it. While she was doing so, it slipped from her hand and fell to the bottom.

In terror and tears, she ran and told her stepmother what had happened.

The woman scolded her. "As you have let the spindle fall into the water," she said, "you may go and get it, for I will not buy another."

The maiden went back to the well, and, hardly knowing what she was about, threw herself into the water to get the spindle.

At first she knew nothing, but as her senses returned, she found herself in a beautiful meadow, where the sun was shining brightly and thousands of flowers were growing.

She walked a long way across the meadow, until she came to a baker's oven which was full of new bread. The loaves cried, "Ah, pull us out! Pull us out, or we shall burn; we have been so long baking!"

Then she stepped near to the oven and with the long bread-shovel took out the loaves.

She walked on after this, and presently came to a tree full of apples. The tree cried, "Shake me, shake me! My apples are ripe!"

She shook the tree till the fruit fell around her like rain, and at last there was not one apple left upon it.

After this she gathered the apples into one large heap, and went on farther.

Soon she came to a small house, and looking at it she saw an old woman peeping out. The woman had such large teeth that the girl was frightened and turned to run away.

The old woman cried after her, "What dost thou fear, dear child? Come and live here with me, and do all the work in the house, and I will make you happy. You must, however, take care to make my bed well, and to shake it with energy, for then the feathers fly about, and in the world they will say it snows, for I am Mother Holly."

As the old woman talked in this kind manner, she won the maiden's heart, so that she agreed to enter her service.

She took care to shake the bed well, so that the feathers might fly down like snowflakes. Therefore she had a very happy life with Mother Holly. She had plenty to eat and drink, and never heard an angry word.

After she had stayed a long time with the kind old woman, she began to feel sad. She could not explain to herself why, till at last she discovered that she was homesick. It seemed to her a thousand times better to go home than to stay with Mother Holly, though the old woman made her so happy.

The longing to go home grew so strong that at last she was obliged to speak.

"Dear Mother Holly," she said, "you have been very kind to me, but I have such sorrow in my heart that I cannot stay here any longer. I must return to my own people."

"Good," said Mother Holly. "I am pleased to hear that you are longing to go home. As you have served me so well and truly, I will show you the way myself."

So she took her by the hand and led her to a broad gateway. The gate was open, and as the young girl passed through there fell upon her a shower of gold. It clung to her dress and remained hanging to it, so that she was covered with gold from head to foot.

"This is your reward for having been so industrious," said the old woman. As she spoke she placed in her hand the spindle which had fallen into the well.

The great gate closed softly and the maiden found herself once more in the world, and not far from her stepmother's house. As she entered the farmyard a cock perched on the wall crowed loudly, and cried, "Our golden lady has come home, I see!"

She went in to her stepmother, and because she was so covered with gold both the mother and sister welcomed her kindly. The maiden told all that had happened to her. And when the mother heard how her wealth had been gained, she was anxious that her own ugly and idle daughter should try her fortune in the same way.

So she made her sit at the well and spin. But the girl, who wished to have all the riches without working for them, did not spin very long at all, for she was daydreaming of all she would buy with her gold.

As soon as she thought enough time had passed, she tossed the spindle into the well. It sank to the bottom, and she sprang in after it, just as her sister had done. And just as her sister had said, she found herself in a beautiful meadow.

She walked for some distance along the same path till she came to the baker's oven. She heard the loaves cry, "Pull us out! Pull us out! or we shall burn; we have been so long baking!"

But the idle girl answered, "No, indeed, I have no wish to soil my hands with your dirty oven." And so she walked on till she came to the apple tree.

"Shake me, shake me!" it cried, "for my apples are ripe."

"I do not agree to that at all," she replied, "for some of the apples might fall on my head." And as she spoke she walked lazily on farther.

When at last she stood before the door of Mother Holly's house, she had no fear of her great teeth, for she had heard all about them from her sister. She walked up to the old woman and offered to be her servant.

Mother Holly accepted the offer of her help. For a whole day the girl was very industrious, as she thought of the gold that was to be showered upon her.

On the second day, however, she gave way to her laziness, and on the third it was worse. Several days passed, and she would not get up early in the morning. The bed was never shaken so that the feathers could fly about.

At last Mother Holly was tired of her, and said she must go away, that her help was not needed.

The lazy girl was quite overjoyed at going, for she thought the golden rain was sure to come when Mother Holly led her to the gate. But as she passed under it, a large kettle full of soot was upset over her.

"That is the reward of your service," said the old woman as she shut the gate.

The idle girl walked home with the soot sticking all over her. As she entered the yard the cock on the wall cried out, "Our sooty young lady has come home, I see."

The soot stuck closely and hung all about her hair and her clothes, and do what she would as long as she lived, it never would come off again.

A Pioneer of Compassion

FRANCIS T. MILLER

Matthew Arnold wrote that "the world is forwarded by having its attention fixed on the best things." Dorothea Dix (1802–1887) lived to fix the world's attention on her crusade to help the suffering, and so led civilization forward. Here is leadership and citizenship born of compassion.

A girl of fourteen years, she found herself facing one of the world's greatest problems—self-support. In addition, she must also support two younger brothers.

"I know I can earn a living," she said. "I can teach the children who are younger than I. I will open a private school."

The child schoolteacher stood before her little pupils with a resoluteness of purpose that inspired them. To give herself an older appearance, she lengthened her skirts and her sleeves. Although scarcely older than the children she taught, her seriousness commanded their respect and affection.

At nineteen, this child teacher was the principal of a boarding school for the daughters of many prominent men of the time. Her strong moral influence had brought her reputation and success.

The early burdens of life wore upon her. Her blue eyes, their warmth chilled by gray, as though sorrow had early crept into her sunny skies, showed failing health, and those about her became greatly worried.

"I do not fear to die," she said, "but I cannot bear the thought of leaving my little brothers. While I live," she added, "I will make myself useful to humanity."

As she looked about her, she found many who were in deeper trouble than herself, some of them with burdens almost too great to bear. She found that there were afflictions in the world as great as physical sickness. There was mental sickness—as hideous in its torment and suffering as any bodily disease.

It was in the year 1841. This young woman was visiting the unfortunate in the House of Correction at East Cambridge, in Massachusetts, when the moans of the wretched came to her ears. Imprisoned in a room, in filth and unspeakable horror, were human beings who had lost their reason, many of them through waywardness and dissipation. Her young heart went out in compassion for them in their misery, and in that compassion burned the fires of justice.

"It is true that they have lost their reason," she admitted, "but they are human beings, they are our fellowmen, and we must protect them."

"This is my mission in life," she decided, and with that decision, she began an investigation of the treatment of the mentally afflicted. She found that civilization looked upon the loss of reason as a curse, and upon its victims as wild beasts, to be chained and bound in irons. Her eyes rested upon sights which she did not know existed in a Christian world. She saw men and women in cages, closets, stalls, and pens. Sometimes they were naked. Often they were cruelly beaten into submission. The gentle voice of this woman cried out in protest.

Hostility and abuse were the response that came back to her.

"It is all humbug," declared the political leaders.

A legislator, after attacking her statements on the floor of the House, declared that he and some of his committee would go to her and refute her allegations. As they entered her home, they were met by the gentle face and voice of this woman.

"We came to inquire about these allegations against our institutions," the leader said coldly.

The woman, smiling, told him of her experiences. She described the misery and fearful sufferings that she had witnessed. As she appealed to the hearts of her visitors, the legislator, after sitting spellbound for an hour and a half, arose and stepping to her side, exclaimed: "Madam, I bid you good night. I do not want, for my part, to hear anything more. The others can stay if they wish to. *I am convinced.* You have conquered me out and out. If you'll come to the House and talk there as you've done here, no man who isn't a brute can withstand you. When a man's convinced, that's enough. The Lord bless you."

The heart of the nation was aroused. Thousands came to her support, while countless others denounced her. She became a political issue in Massachusetts, and the legislature, after a heated discussion, passed an appropriation to remove the insane from the jails to institutions where they could receive mental treatment.

The lifework of the woman had now just begun. She went from Massachusetts to Rhode Island, and on and on until she had visited all the states east of the Rocky Mountains. Everywhere her eyes rested upon the same inhuman conditions that she had found in Massachusetts. In the treatment of its mental unfortunates, civilization had become savage. She visited the prisons and almshouses. Her appeals to humanity were overpowering. As she journeyed through the country, she wore a simple dress of plain gray for traveling, and appeared in severe black on public occasions, frequently wearing a shawl about her shoulders.

One day, while in Rhode Island, she went to see a millionaire who had no special fondness for benevolence. He tried to baffle her with commonplace generalities, which she met with kindness. At last, rising with commanding dignity, she announced the purpose of her interview.

The financier, hardened though he was by a life devoted to mere moneymaking, listened. Her low-voiced eloquence appealed to him.

"God will not hold us guiltless for the neglect of one of the least of His creatures," she declared.

"But what would you have me do?" inquired the rich man.

"Give fifty thousand dollars toward a new asylum for the insane," she answered.

"I will do it," he replied.

Some months later this woman, now a broken-down invalid, weakened by her travels and labors, stood before Congress. For six years she pleaded with the government for better laws for the insane, and at last her wisdom and humanity conquered the hearts and minds of the statesmen.

It was 1854. A bill before Congress was for an appropriation of 12,225,000 acres of public lands—about 20,000 square miles—to be apportioned among the states for the care of the insane, allowing the odd 225,000 acres for the deaf. The bill swept the Senate by more than a two-thirds majority, and passed the House by a plurality of fourteen.

The woman wept with thanksgiving.

"I must resist the deep sympathies of my heart," said President Pierce, as he returned the bill to the Senate without his signature and bearing his veto.

The worn woman was crushed by this defeat, and she was taken across the seas to recover her lost energy and strength. But her life mission weighed upon her, and, immediately upon her arrival in Scotland, she began to work for the remodeling of its lunacy laws. Some officials resented the intrusion, and moved to oppose her. Refusing to give up, she turned toward London for help, and her efforts led Parliament to rise to the defense of mental sufferers and revise its laws on principles of Christian brotherhood.

The conquest of civilization by an invalid American woman was now well begun. When she entered Italy, in 1856, she found the prisons and hospitals of ancient Rome in confusion and disorder. A few days later she stood before Pope Pius IX, and appealed to his beneficence. He expressed himself surprised and shocked at the details of her recital, and, on the following day he fell unawares on the officials and personally investigated the conditions in the prisons, which he found to be only too true. The result was the purchase of land and the establishment of a retreat for the mentally afflicted of the great metropolis of the ancient civilization.

Cries of distress from all parts of Europe called this American woman from Rome. In Athens, Constantinople, Moscow, St. Petersburg, Vienna, Paris, Florence—everywhere she carried the new light of science to those who were suffering under the shadow of a great affliction.

The gloom of a great civil war fell upon her beloved America. And as the cannon boomed, under the flag that she loved, she carried the compassion of her heart to the wounded and dying and offered her life to her country as a superintendent of nurses. It was through her efforts that many monuments were erected to the Union soldiers who had fallen on the field or perished in the prison pens or hospital wards. It was this woman who brought to the army and navy compassion for the heroes who had become insane in the service. It was this good Samaritan whose name ran through every state in the Union, across Canada, and around the world—appealing to the universal heart of humanity.

And yet, this great woman, whose soul was overflowing with love for all humanity, was herself a homeless wanderer. This life spent for the happiness of others was poured out in loneliness and suffering.

One day a white-haired lady of about eighty years of age, plainly dressed, and bent by the weight of years, retired to the mental hospital at Trenton, New Jersey.

"This is my firstborn child," she said. "It is here that I want to die."

Five years later this beneficent life passed away so quietly that the world hardly knew she was gone. Those for whom she had labored did not know, and could not love. Over her lifeless form they could not grieve; they were in darkness that knows no grief.

But there is One who knows and One who loves, and to those all-embracing arms she passed with the tender words: "Come, ye blessed of my Father, inherit the kingdom prepared for you from the foundation of the world, for I was hungry and ye gave me meat; I was thirsty and ye gave me drink; I was a stranger and ye took me in; naked and ye clothed me; sick and in prison and ye visited me."

And as the light of His face falls upon her, we can hear the echo of the voice of Him Who gave His life to save humanity: "Inasmuch as ye have done it unto one of the least of these My brethren, ye have done it unto Me."

This is a story of the heroism of peace—the story of Dorothea Lynde Dix, one of the noblest of American women.

Sacajawea

FRANCIS T. MILLER

Sacajawea (whose name means "bird woman") helped lead the way on one of the greatest overland adventures in American history. Here is the kind of courage and perseverance that moves the world along.

It was a full hundred years ago that the tribe of Indians known to history as the Shoshones made their home a little west of the Rocky Mountains, or, as the range was called by them, the "Bitter Root Mountains." Here it was that Sacajawea and her little friends played their childish games, with no thought of anything outside of their own lives. It was not always playtime among the children; from infancy they were taught to labor with their hands, and their education in other respects was not neglected. At a surprisingly early age, they became skilled in the use of the bow, and they were sent into the forest to gather herbs and roots, for medicine and food.

One day, into this peaceful valley, without warning, the powerful Minnetarees, or Blackfeet, tribe swept down in battle array. Devastation followed in their wake. Many of the Shoshones were killed and many were carried away into captivity. Among the captives was little Sacajawea. Away over the mountains she was borne into the far, far east. Naturally alert and observing, the little maid absorbed every incident of this new experience, so that in after years, when traveling back over this same country, she was able to recognize most of the landmarks on the way.

Sacajawea was sold as a slave when she reached the east. A French Canadian, named Charboneau, who was an Indian interpreter, bought her when she was only five years old. When she was fourteen he made her his wife, and a year later a son was born to her.

It was about this time that American explorers were looking toward the great, mysterious region in the Far West. They believed that it was a land of great wealth, and they longed to plant the American flag on its mountains. Men called them foolhardy and said that it was a worthless jungle of forests and rocks and beasts, that it was not worth the risk of life it would take to survey it.

But there were two explorers—Lewis and Clark—who were willing to undertake it. Shortly after starting on their hazardous journey, they entered the little Indian village of Mandan. There they found Charboneau, who could talk many tongues. Their eyes fell also upon the little Indian mother, Sacajawea. Charboneau told them that his Indian wife knew the whole country, and was a natural guide. Sacajawea, in her native tongue, told them how she knew the trails; how she could take them through country never before traveled by the feet of white men; and how she could show them the beauties of the land of her birth, with its towering blue mountains, capped with snow, and its golden valleys, its gorges and rivers, its glittering sands, and its thousand and one beauties that have since given it the name of the "Garden of the Gods."

"We will go with you," said Charboneau and Sacajawea.

And so it was that when that expedition, which opened up the western domain of America, started on the most perilous portion of its journey, Sacajawea was a guide and Charboneau an interpreter. Sacajawea strapped her two-month-old baby on her shoulders, and carried him in this snug pocket throughout the entire journey. She was the only woman in the party and she rendered vital service to the explorers.

Into the heart of the wilderness they plunged. When all signs of human life were left far behind them, and there were none to beckon them onward, then it was that the native instinct of this woman came to their assistance. At times sickness or starvation seemed imminent. Then Sacajawea would go into the woods, where in secret she gathered herbs to cure each ailment, or dug roots, from which she prepared savory dishes for their meals.

The men marveled at the courage and ingenuity of this faithful pilot. Burdened though she was with the care of the young child, she never seemed to feel fatigue. No complaint ever escaped her lips. Patient, plucky, and determined, she was a constant source of inspiration to the explorers.

The baby laughed and cooed as the wonders of the world were revealed to it. With all its mother's fearlessness, it swung calmly on her faithful back while she climbed over jagged precipices and forded swiftly running rivers.

One day a little incident occurred, which illustrates the true character of this woman. While making their way along one of the rivers, her husband, in a clumsy attempt to readjust things, overturned the canoe containing every article necessary for the journey. Without a moment's hesitation Sacajawea plunged into the river, risking her own life and that of the infant strapped to her. Clothing, bundles, and many valuable documents of the expedition were thus rescued. If these things had been lost, the party would have been obliged to retrace its steps hundreds of miles, in order to replace them. This is, indeed, the heroism that makes history. The alertness of Sacajawea's native instinct and her faithful kindness worked inestimable benefit to our nation. In gratitude for her great services, the explorers named after her the next river that they discovered.

Some months later, scenes began to take on a familiar aspect to Sacajawea, and she showed signs of elation. She pointed out old landmarks which indicated that she was nearing her old home. They at last pitched their camp where years before, as a little child, she had been taken captive. Here she soon found old friends, and to her unspeakable delight she discovered among them her own brother. Wrapped closely in his arms, she sobbed out all the sorrow which had been bound up in her heart for so many years. From him she learned that all of her family had died, except two of her brothers and a son of her eldest sister.

Sacajawea was at home again. Now and then little snatches of songs of contentment reached the ears of the members of the great expedition. They might naturally have thought that now it would not be easy for the girl to attend them on their westward journey. But if they entertained this fear, they misjudged

Sacajawea. She never flinched from her first intention, and cheerfully left her long-lost friends to plunge once more into the unbroken and unknown forests beyond the Rockies. The solitude was enough to shake a strong man's courage. Never a sound was to be heard except the dismal, distant howl of wild beasts and occasionally the war cry of savages, but Sacajawea did not falter.

Thus they plodded overland, ever westward, until the end of the journey drew near. They made a camp inland, leaving Sacajawea in its protection, and then pushed to the coast.

"It is the Pacific!" they cried at last.

In their enthusiasm, the explorers forgot the brave Sacajawea. They talked of the Pacific in the camp, but did not allow her to go to the coast until she pleaded with them to let her gaze upon the waters.

Then she was satisfied. She had seen the "great waters" and the "fish," as she called the whale which spouted on its surface.

It was an epoch-making journey, in which the path was blazed by a woman. It rivaled the great explorations of Stanley and Livingstone in daring, and far exceeded them in importance. It was an expedition that moved the world along; that pushed the boundary of the United States from the Mississippi to the Pacific; that gave us the breadth of the continent from ocean to ocean; that led to the command of its rivers and harbors, the wealth of its mountains, plains, and valleys—a dominion vast enough for the ambitions of kings.

Second Message to Congress

ABRAHAM LINCOLN

*In December 1862, with the Northern war effort seemingly grind-
ing to a halt and public opinion turning against him, Abraham
Lincoln resolutely wrote Congress that the federal government now
faced two moral and political obligations: preserve the Union, and free
the slaves. In Lincoln's mind, the two objectives had, at this point,
become inseparable. He made his plea despite the protestations of some
advisors who called his emancipation plans reckless and destructive.
Here is the voice of a leader asking his fellow countrymen to cast off the
prejudices of generations and follow the dictates of right and reason.
One month later, Lincoln would sign the Emancipation Proclamation.*

A nation may be said to consist of its territory, its people,
and its laws. The territory is the only part which is of certain durability. "One generation passeth away, and another generation cometh, but the earth abideth forever." It is of the first
importance to duly consider, and estimate, this ever-enduring
part. That portion of the earth's surface which is owned and
inhabited by the people of the United States, is well adapted to

be the home of one national family; and it is not well adapted for two, or more. Its vast extent, and its variety of climate and productions, are of advantage, in this age, for one people, whatever they might have been in former ages. Steam, telegraphs, and intelligence, have brought these, to be an advantageous combination, for one united people.

In the inaugural address I briefly pointed out the total inadequacy of disunion, as a remedy for the differences between the people of the two sections. I did so in language which I cannot improve, and which, therefore, I beg to repeat:

"One section of our country believes slavery is *right*, and ought to be extended, while the other believes it is *wrong*, and ought not to be extended. This is the only substantial dispute. . . . Physically speaking, we cannot separate. We cannot remove our respective sections from each other, nor build an impassable wall between them. A husband and wife may be divorced, and go out of the presence, and beyond the reach of each other; but the different parts of our country cannot do this. They cannot but remain face-to-face; and intercourse, either amicable or hostile, must continue between them. Is it possible, then, to make that intercourse more advantageous, or more satisfactory, *after* separation than *before?* Can aliens make treaties, easier than friends can make laws? Can treaties be more faithfully enforced between aliens, than laws can among friends? Suppose you go to war, you cannot fight always; and when, after much loss on both sides, and no gain on either, you cease fighting, the identical old questions, as to terms of intercourse, are again upon you. . . ."

If there ever could be a proper time for mere catch arguments, that time surely is not now. In times like the present, men should utter nothing for which they would not willingly be responsible through time and in eternity. . . .

I do not forget the gravity which should characterize a paper addressed to the Congress of the nation by the Chief Magistrate of the nation. Nor do I forget that some of you are my seniors, nor that many of you have more experience than I, in the conduct of public affairs. Yet I trust that in view of the great responsibility resting upon me, you will perceive no want of respect to yourselves, in any undue earnestness I may seem to display. . . .

The dogmas of the quiet past are inadequate to the stormy present. The occasion is piled high with difficulty, and we must rise with the occasion. As our case is new, so we must think anew, and act anew. We must disenthrall ourselves, and then we shall save our country.

Fellow citizens, *we* cannot escape history. We of this Congress and this administration will be remembered in spite of ourselves. No personal significance, or insignificance, can spare one or another of us. The fiery trial through which we pass will light us down, in honor or dishonor, to the latest generation. We *say* we are for the Union. The world will not forget that we say this. We know how to save the Union. The world knows we do know how to save it. We—even *we here*—hold the power, and bear the responsibility. In *giving* freedom to the *slave,* we *assure* freedom to the *free*—honorable alike in what we give, and what we preserve. We shall nobly save, or meanly lose, the last best hope of earth. Other means may succeed; this could not fail. The way is plain, peaceful, generous, just—a way which, if followed, the world will forever applaud, and God must forever bless.

The Sleeping Sentinel

ADAPTED FROM ALBERT BLAISDELL
AND FRANCIS BALL

This story, based on an incident that occurred early in the Civil War, entered the corpus of Lincoln lore when it was set to verse and read in the U.S. Senate chamber before an audience that included President Lincoln himself. It reminds us that good leaders set high but reasonable expectations for those who would follow.

On a rainy morning in September 1861, during the first year of the Civil War, a group of Union soldiers came to the White House to plead for the life of one of their friends. They were granted an audience with President Lincoln himself, and in faltering words they told why they had come.

The soldiers were part of the Third Vermont Regiment, which was made up mostly of farm boys from the Green Mountains. Since their arrival in Washington they had been stationed at Chain Bridge, a few miles above the city. The bridge was of vital importance since Confederate forces occupied the hills on the opposite side of the Potomac River. The soldiers' orders were strict: Any sentinel caught sleeping at his post was to be shot within twenty-four hours.

According to the soldiers' story, a boy named William Scott had enlisted in Company K. He had been on duty one night, and the following night had taken the place of a comrade too sick to stand guard. The third night he had been called out on guard duty yet again. The young fellow could not keep awake for three nights in a row. When the relief guard came around, he was found asleep. Arrested, tried, and found guilty, he was sentenced to be shot.

"William Scott, sir, is as brave a soldier as there is in your army," the Green Mountain Boys told Lincoln. "He is no coward. It's not right to shoot him like a traitor and bury him like a dog."

Later in the day President Lincoln rode from the White House in the direction of Chain Bridge. Within a day or so the newspapers reported that a soldier sentenced to death for sleeping at his post had been pardoned by the president, and had returned to his regiment.

It was a long time before Scott would speak of his interview with President Lincoln. One day he told a comrade the whole story.

"I knew the president at once," he said, "by a Lincoln medal I had long worn. I was scared at first, for I had never talked with a great man before. He asked me all about the folks at home, my brothers and sisters, and where I went to school, and how I liked it. Then he asked me about my mother. I showed him her picture. He said that if he were in my place he would try to make a fond mother happy, and never cause her a sorrow or a tear.

"'My boy,' he said, 'you are not going to be shot. You are going back to your regiment. I have been put to a good deal of trouble on your account. Now what I want to know is how you are going to pay me back. My bill is a large one, and there is only one man in all the world who can pay it. His name is William Scott. If from this day you will promise to do your whole duty as a soldier, then the debt will be paid. Will you make that promise and try to keep it?'"

Gladly the young Vermont soldier made the promise, and well did he keep it. From that day William Scott became a model man of his regiment. He was never absent from a roll call. He was always on hand if there was any hard work to do. He worked nights in the hospital, nursing the sick and wounded, because it trained him to keep awake. He made a record for himself on picket duty, and distinguished himself as a scout.

Sometime after this the Third Vermont went into one of its many hard battles. They were ordered to attack the Confederate lines, and William Scott fell in the enemy volley.

His comrades caught him up, carried him bleeding and dying from the field, and laid him on a cot.

"Tell the president I have tried to be a good soldier, and true to the flag," he said.

Then, making a last effort, with his dying breath he prayed for Abraham Lincoln.

Company K buried William Scott in a grove just in the rear of the camp, at the foot of a big oak tree. Deep into the oak they cut the initials "W. S." and under it the words "A Brave Soldier."

Sojourner Truth

FROM *THE NARRATIVE
OF SOJOURNER TRUTH*

*In 1843, a former slave born with the name Isabella left New York
City with a bag of clothes, twenty-five cents, and a new name—
Sojourner Truth—a name she chose, she said, because God had told
her to travel the land, declaring the truth. For the remainder of her life,
she spoke out loudly and fearlessly on behalf of her causes, which
included the abolition of slavery, equal rights for women, and education for freed slaves. Here is someone born into the worst of conditions
who nonetheless rose to lead others to better lives. The passage below
comes from* The Narrative of Sojourner Truth, *published in 1875.
The incident described here took place in Washington, D.C., shortly
after the Civil War.*

While Sojourner was engaged in the hospital, she often
had occasion to procure articles from various parts of the
city for the sick soldiers, and would sometimes be obliged to
walk a long distance, carrying her burdens upon her arm. She

would gladly have availed herself of the street cars; but, although there was on each track one car called the Jim Crow car, nominally for the accommodation of colored people, yet should they succeed in getting on at all they would seldom have more than the privilege of standing, as the seats were usually filled with white folks. Unwilling to submit to this state of things, she complained to the president of the street railroad, who ordered the Jim Crow car to be taken off. A law was now passed giving the colored people equal car privileges with the white.

Not long after this, Sojourner, having occasion to ride, signaled the car, but neither conductor nor driver noticed her. Soon another followed, and she raised her hand again, but they also turned away. She then gave three tremendous yelps, "I want to ride! *I want to ride!* I WANT TO RIDE!!!" Consternation seized the passing crowd—people, carriages, go-carts of every description stood still. The car was effectually blocked up, and before it could move on, Sojourner had jumped aboard. Then there arose a great shout from the crowd, "Ha! ha! ha!! She has beaten him," etc. The angry conductor told her to go forward where the horses were, or he would put her out. Quietly seating herself, she informed him that she was a passenger. "Go forward where the horses are, or I will throw you out," said he in a menacing voice. She told him that she was neither a Marylander nor a Virginian to fear his threats; but was from the Empire State of New York, and knew the laws as well as he did.

Several soldiers were in the car, and when other passengers came in, they related the circumstance and said, "You ought to have heard that old woman talk to the conductor." Sojourner rode farther than she needed to go; for a ride was so rare a privilege that she determined to make the most of it. She left the car feeling very happy, and said, "Bless God! I have had a ride."

Returning one day from the Orphans' Home at Georgetown, she hastened to reach a car; but they paid no attention to her signal, and kept ringing a bell that they might not hear her. She ran after it, and when it stopped to take other passengers, she succeeded in overtaking it and, getting in, said to the conductor, "It is a shame to make a lady run so." He told her if she said another word, he would put her off the car, and came forward as if to execute his threat. She replied, "If you attempt that, it will cost you more than your car and horses are worth." A gentleman of dignified and commanding manner, wearing a general's uniform, interfered in her behalf, and the conductor gave her no further trouble.

Saint Francis and the Wolf

RETOLD BY FRANCES DADMUN

Sometimes the courage to lead comes from deep faith.

S aint Francis lived several hundred years ago in Italy. All the
clothes he owned were a brown robe with a rope for a belt,
and leather sandals. He generally went bareheaded unless the
sun was hot or the rain heavy, and then he drew the hood of his
robe over his head and went his way very comfortably. There
were years when he had no home, but it made no difference, for
he was happy anywhere. Every man was his friend and even the
wild beasts trusted him.

One day, when Saint Francis was out for a walk, he saw a
little town perched on a hill.

"There is Gubbio," he said to some friends who were walking with him. "I have good friends there. We must go up and
make them a visit."

There was a high stone wall all about Gubbio which you
couldn't possibly have climbed because it was higher than a

house and very steep. People went in and out of a great gate which was locked every night to keep out robbers, but in the daytime it was generally wide open.

This morning, when Saint Francis and his friends came to the gate, they were surprised to find it closed. They had to knock several times before anyone opened it.

"What is the trouble, good brother, that the gate is shut?" asked Saint Francis.

"It's a great Wolf!" said the man, who was a peasant. "A huge fierce fellow he is, too. He eats men. He is so bold that we have seen him at this very gate where you came in, just now. It's a mercy that he didn't eat you."

"And no one dares go outside?" said Saint Francis.

"No one," said the peasant.

By this time, the street was full of people who had heard the knocking at the gate. They looked so frightened and wild-eyed that Saint Francis was sorry for them.

"Come, brothers," he said to his companions, "we will go out and see this Wolf."

The people cried out, "No, no!" until the narrow street echoed. Those who were nearest clutched the skirts of Saint Francis's brown robe.

"Yes, yes!" said Saint Francis, "I am not afraid of the Wolf. He will be my friend."

The people knew that Saint Francis meant what he said and opened the gates, but their fingers trembled as they drew back the bolts.

Saint Francis and his companions went straight to the hills where the Wolf was hiding and the people of Gubbio followed at a safe distance. But Saint Francis was fearless. He put his trust in God.

So he left even his faithful companions and went on alone. And then he saw the Wolf, running swiftly with head low and mouth partly open. Saint Francis stood still.

"Come here, Brother Wolf," said Saint Francis. "In the name of Jesus, do not hurt anybody."

The Wolf closed his mouth, stopped running. He crept forward and lay down at the feet of Saint Francis.

"Brother Wolf," said Saint Francis, "you have done great harm in these parts, killing God's creatures—not only beasts but people, whom God made in His image! All people cry against you and all this land hates you. But I, Brother Wolf, would make peace between you and the people. Do no more harm and they will forgive you, and neither people nor dogs shall torment you anymore."

The Wolf wagged his tail and his head drooped. He knew what it was to be tormented by people and dogs. He, as well as the people, had had a hard time.

"Brother Wolf," said Saint Francis, and he looked at the poor, lean sides where every rib showed, "if you are willing to be peaceable, I promise you that you will be fed as long as you live; for I know well that you have done all this harm because you were hungry. But since I do this for you, Brother Wolf, will you promise me that you will never again hurt either an animal or a human being?"

The Wolf bowed his head, but Saint Francis wanted more.

"Brother Wolf, you must give a pledge for your promise, that I may surely trust you."

Saint Francis stretched forth his right hand. The people gave a great cry of wonder, for the Wolf lifted his right paw and meekly placed it in the hand of Saint Francis, giving all the promise he could.

"Brother Wolf," said Saint Francis, "come with me and let us repeat this promise before all the people."

The Wolf followed Saint Francis back to the town, and as the news spread, men and women, young and old, big and little, trooped to the marketplace to see the Wolf with Saint Francis. When everybody in town was surely there, Saint Francis—and you know by this time that he was a real saint—spoke to the people.

"Listen, my brothers. Brother Wolf, here before you, has promised me to make peace with you and not to trouble you again in any way; and you are to promise him that you will give him all he needs to eat."

The people all shouted at once that they would feed their new friend regularly.

"And you, Brother Wolf," said Saint Francis, "do you promise to observe this treaty of peace that you will harm neither people nor animals nor any creature?"

The Wolf kneeled and bowed his head. He wriggled gently, he wagged his tail and lifted his ears, showing as plainly as a wolf could that he would keep the treaty.

"But, Brother Wolf," urged Saint Francis, "I wish you to promise me before all these people as you did outside the gate, and let me promise in turn never to break my word to you."

The Wolf understood, for he lifted his paw and placed it in the hand of Saint Francis. Once more the people cried out, this time with joy, and they thanked God for sending them Saint Francis, who had saved them from the mouth of the Wolf. No one knows what the Wolf thought, but we can guess that he was thankful, too; for he would never have been so fierce if he had not nearly starved to death in the first place.

He lived two years in Gubbio and went among the houses from door to door, without hurting anyone. He was fed by the people most politely, and not even a dog barked at him. After two years, Brother Wolf died of old age, and everyone was sorry. He was not only loved for his own sake but was always reminding the people of their dear friend, Saint Francis.

Saint George and the Dragon

RETOLD BY J. BERG ESENWEIN AND MARIETTA STOCKARD

"Somewhere perhaps there is trouble and fear," Saint George says in this story before riding off to "find work which only a knight can do." Here we see the course of a morally ambitious conscience, habitually searching to aid others. Such people who go out of their way to help are sometimes called knights, saints, and philanthropists; sometimes they are called ministers, teachers, coaches, policemen, and parents.

Long ago, when the knights lived in the land, there was one knight whose name was Sir George. He was not only braver than all the rest, but he was so noble, kind, and good that the people came to call him Saint George.

No robbers ever dared to trouble the people who lived near his castle, and all the wild animals were killed or driven away, so the little children could play even in the woods without being afraid.

One day Saint George rode throughout the country.

Everywhere he saw the men busy at their work in the fields, the women singing at work in their homes, and the little children shouting at their play.

"These people are all safe and happy. They need me no more," said Saint George.

"But somewhere perhaps there is trouble and fear. There may be someplace where little children cannot play in safety, some woman may have been carried away from her home—perhaps there are even dragons left to be slain. Tomorrow I shall ride away and never stop until I find work which only a knight can do."

Early the next morning Saint George put on his helmet and all his shining armor, and fastened his sword at his side. Then he mounted his great white horse and rode out from his castle gate. Down the steep, rough road he went, sitting straight and tall, and looking brave and strong as a knight should look.

On through the little village at the foot of the hill and out across the country he rode. Everywhere he saw rich fields filled with waving grain, everywhere there was peace and plenty.

He rode on and on until at last he came into a part of the country he had never seen before. He noticed that there were no men working in the fields. The houses which he passed stood silent and empty. The grass along the roadside was scorched as if a fire had passed over it. A field of wheat was all trampled and burned.

Saint George drew up his horse, and looked carefully about him. Everywhere there was silence and desolation. "What can be the dreadful thing which has driven all the people from their homes? I must find out, and give them help if I can," he said.

But there was no one to ask, so Saint George rode forward

until at last far in the distance he saw the walls of a city. "Here surely I shall find someone who can tell me the cause of all this," he said, so he rode more swiftly toward the city.

Just then the great gate opened and Saint George saw crowds of people standing inside the wall. Some of them were weeping, all of them seemed afraid. As Saint George watched, he saw a beautiful maiden dressed in white, with a girdle of scarlet about her waist, pass through the gate alone. The gate clanged shut and the maiden walked along the road, weeping bitterly. She did not see Saint George, who was riding quickly toward her.

"Maiden, why do you weep?" he asked as he reached her side.

She looked up at Saint George sitting there on his horse, so straight and tall and beautiful. "Oh, Sir Knight!" she cried, "ride quickly from this place. You know not the danger you are in!"

"Danger!" said Saint George. "Do you think a knight would flee from danger? Besides, you, a fair girl, are here alone. Think you a knight would leave you so? Tell me your trouble that I may help you."

"No! No!" she cried. "Hasten away. You would only lose your life. There is a terrible dragon near. He may come at any moment. One breath would destroy you if he found you here. Go! Go quickly!"

"Tell me more of this," said Saint George sternly. "Why are you here alone to meet this dragon? Are there no *men* left in yon city?"

"Oh," said the maiden, "my father, the king, is old and feeble. He has only me to help him take care of his people. This terrible dragon has driven them from their homes, carried away their cattle, and ruined their crops. They have all come within the walls of the city for safety. For weeks now the dragon has come to the very gates of the city. We have been forced to give him two sheep each day for his breakfast.

"Yesterday there were no sheep left to give, so he said that unless a young maiden were given him today he would break down the walls and destroy the city. The people cried to my father to save them, but he could do nothing. I am going to give myself to the dragon. Perhaps if he has me, the Princess, he may spare our people."

"Lead the way, brave princess. Show me where this monster may be found."

When the princess saw Saint George's flashing eyes and great, strong arm as he drew forth his sword, she felt afraid no more. Turning, she led the way to a shining pool.

"There's where he stays," she whispered. "See, the water moves. He is waking."

Saint George saw the head of the dragon lifted from the pool. Fold on fold he rose from the water. When he saw Saint George he gave a roar of rage and plunged toward him. The smoke and flames flew from his nostrils, and he opened his great jaws as if to swallow both the knight and his horse.

Saint George shouted and, waving his sword above his head, rode at the dragon. Quick and hard came the blows from Saint George's sword. It was a terrible battle.

At last the dragon was wounded. He roared with pain and plunged at Saint George, opening his great mouth close to the brave knight's head.

Saint George looked carefully, then struck with all his strength straight down through the dragon's throat, and he fell at the horse's feet—dead.

Then Saint George shouted for joy at his victory. He called to the princess. She came and stood beside him.

"Give me the girdle from about your waist, O Princess," said Saint George.

The princess gave him her girdle and Saint George bound it around the dragon's neck, and they pulled the dragon after them by that little silken ribbon back to the city so that all of the people could see that the dragon could never harm them again.

When they saw Saint George bringing the princess back in safety and knew that the dragon was slain, they threw open the gates of the city and sent up great shouts of joy.

The king heard them and came out from his palace to see why the people were shouting.

When he saw his daughter safe he was the happiest of them all.

"O brave knight," he said, "I am old and weak. Stay here and help me guard my people from harm."

"I'll stay as long as ever you have need of me," Saint George answered.

So he lived in the palace and helped the old king take care of his people, and when the old king died, Saint George was made king in his stead. The people felt happy and safe so long as they had such a brave and good man for their king.

Saint Martin and the Beggar

ADAPTED FROM A RETELLING
BY PEGGY WEBLING

Born around the year 316 in the Roman province of Pannonia (Hungary), Martin was forced into military service at the age of fifteen by his father, an army officer. It was in about 337 while he was stationed in Amiens, France, that the famous incident described below is said to have occurred. Martin converted to Christianity a short time later and began a long career of serving his God and fellowman, becoming Bishop of Tours and founding the renowned abbey of Marmoutier. Today he is a patron saint of France, and his symbol of a sword cutting a cloak in half is a widely loved reminder of the power of sharing.

It is a bright, frosty morning on a busy street in the old town of Amiens in France, hundreds of years ago. People are trudging to work or bustling to the marketplace. Here and there little crowds gather to talk together, while boys and girls run along, laughing, playing, behaving very much as they do today.

A young scholar passes by, looking lost in thought, then a rich lady with a servant at her heels, then a prosperous merchant with his clerk beside him listening meekly to his master's orders.

In a shadow of the city wall, as unheeded as a mound of dust, stands a poor, ragged beggar, shivering with cold, one feeble hand stretched out for alms. The people pass him by, most of them ignoring him altogether, some with a glance of half-contemptuous pity, or even disgust.

His pleading voice is so weak that it fades away. He is utterly despised.

Suddenly there is the ring of horses' hooves on the hard road, and a little band of the Emperor's soldiers canter down the street. They are talking merrily among themselves. Their swords, their big spurs, and the trappings of their steeds glisten in the sunshine. They are leaving for a distant city, and carelessly glance at the people who stand still to watch them ride by, admiring their youth and gallant bearing.

As they pass by the shadow of the city wall, one of the young soldiers in the rear of the troop reins in his horse. His face changes when he notices something.

It is nothing to attract anyone's attention, only a shuddering beggar with outstretched hands and a haggard, starving face. But when Martin sees the other soldiers pass by the poor creature without a glance, he wonders if perhaps this man has been left for him to help.

There is no money in young Martin's purse—he has given it all away in charity or farewell gifts. But he feels he must do something.

Then an idea flashes into his head, suggested by the cold

wind that whistles through the air. He loosens the great, warm military cloak hanging from his shoulders and holds it up with one hand. With the other hand he draws his sword, and cuts the cloth right down the middle. Then he leans from the saddle and with a word of sympathy drops one half of the garment over the shoulders of the wretched beggar. Then he sheaths his sword, tosses the rest of the cloak back over his own shoulders, and gallops after his companions.

Some of the other young officers break out in laughter and jests as Martin joins them, with his strip of torn cloak fluttering behind him. But others wish they had thought of doing what he has done.

And that night Martin had a dream in which he saw Jesus in heaven, surrounded by a company of angels. In this vision, the Lord was wearing one half of a cloak, and He showed it to the angels, saying, "See, here is the garment Martin gave to Me."

Surrender at Appomattox

HORACE PORTER

Great leaders display certain virtues when the end comes, no matter what the outcome. Here is grace in victory and grace in defeat. The account comes from an eyewitness at Appomattox Courthouse, Virginia, where on April 9, 1865, General Robert E. Lee surrendered the Confederate Army of Northern Virginia to General Ulysses S. Grant, effectively ending the Civil War.

General Grant began the conversation by saying: "I met you once before, General Lee, while we were serving in Mexico, when you came over from General Scott's headquarters to visit Garland's brigade, to which I then belonged. I have always remembered your appearance, and I think I should have recognized you anywhere." "Yes," replied General Lee, "I know I met you on that occasion, and I have often thought of it and tried to recollect how you looked, but I have never been able to recall a single feature." After some further mention of Mexico, General Lee said: "I suppose, General Grant, that the object of our present meeting is fully understood. I asked to see you to ascertain upon what terms you would receive the surrender of my army." General Grant replied: "The terms I propose are those stated substantially in my letter of yesterday—that is, the officers and men surrendered to be paroled and disqualified from taking up arms again until properly exchanged, and all arms, ammunition, and supplies to be delivered up as captured property." Lee nodded an assent, and said: "Those are about the conditions which I expected would be proposed." General Grant then continued: "Yes, I think our correspondence indicated pretty clearly the action that would be taken at our meeting; and I hope it may lead to a general suspension of hostilities and be the means of preventing any further loss of life."

Lee inclined his head as indicating his accord with this wish, and General Grant then went on to talk at some length in a very pleasant vein about the prospects of peace. Lee was evidently anxious to proceed to the formal work of the surrender, and he brought the subject up again by saying: "I presume, General Grant, we have both carefully considered the proper steps to be taken, and I would suggest that you commit to writing the terms you have proposed, so that they may be formally acted upon."

"Very well," replied General Grant, "I will write them out." And calling for his manifold order book, he opened it on the table before him and proceeded to write the terms. The leaves had been so prepared that three impressions of the writing were made. He wrote very rapidly, and did not pause until he had finished the sentence ending with "officers appointed by me to receive them." Then he looked toward Lee, and his eyes seemed to be resting on the handsome sword that hung at that officer's side. He said afterward that this set him to thinking that it would be an unnecessary humiliation to require the officers to surrender their swords, and a great hardship to deprive them of their personal baggage and horses, and after a short pause he wrote the sentence: "This will not embrace the side arms of the officers, nor their private horses or baggage." When he had finished the letter he called Colonel (afterward General) Ely S. Parker, one of the military secretaries on the staff, to his side and looked it over with him and directed him as they went along to interline six or seven words and to strike out the word "their," which had been repeated. When this had been done, he handed the book to General Lee and asked him to read over the letter. . . .

Lee took it and laid it on the table beside him, while he drew from his pocket a pair of steel-rimmed spectacles and wiped the glasses carefully with his handkerchief. Then he crossed his legs, adjusted the spectacles very slowly and deliberately, took up the draft of the letter, and proceeded to read it attentively. . . .

When Lee came to the sentence about the officers' side arms, private horses, and baggage, he showed for the first time during the reading of the letter a slight change of countenance, and was evidently touched by this act of generosity. It was doubtless the condition mentioned to which he particularly alluded when he looked toward General Grant as he finished reading and said with some degree of warmth in his manner: "This will have a very happy effect upon my army."

General Grant then said: "Unless you have some suggestions to make in regard to the form in which I have stated the terms, I will have a copy of the letter made in ink and sign it."

"There is one thing I would like to mention," Lee replied

after a short pause. "The cavalrymen and artillerists own their own horses in our army. Its organization in this respect differs from that of the United States." This expression attracted the notice of our officers present, as showing how firmly the conviction was grounded in his mind that we were two distinct countries. He continued: "I would like to understand whether these men will be permitted to retain their horses."

"You will find that the terms as written do not allow this," General Grant replied; "only the officers are permitted to take their private property."

Lee read over the second page of the letter again, and then said: "No, I see the terms do not allow it; that is clear." His face showed plainly that he was quite anxious to have this concession made, and Grant said very promptly and without giving Lee time to make a direct request: "Well, the subject is quite new to me. Of course I did not know that any private soldiers owned their animals, but I think this will be the last battle of the war—I sincerely hope so—and that the surrender of this army will be followed soon by that of all the others, and I take it that most of the men in the ranks are small farmers, and as the country has been so raided by the two armies, it is doubtful whether they will be able to put in a crop to carry themselves and their families through the next winter without the aid of the horses they are now riding, and I will arrange it in this way: I will not change the terms as now written, but I will instruct the officers I shall appoint to receive the paroles to let all the men who claim to own a horse or mule take the animals home with them to work their little farms." (This expression has been quoted in various forms and has been the subject of some dispute. I give the exact words used.)

Lee now looked greatly relieved, and though anything but a demonstrative man, he gave every evidence of his appreciation of this concession, and said, "This will have the best possible effect upon the men. It will be very gratifying and will do much toward conciliating our people." He handed the draft of the terms back to General Grant, who called Colonel T. S. Bowers of the staff to him and directed him to make a copy in ink. . . .

General Lee now took the initiative again in leading the conversation back into business channels. He said: "I have a thousand or more of your men as prisoners, General Grant, a number of them officers whom we have required to march along with us for several days. I shall be glad to send them into your lines as soon as it can be arranged, for I have no provisions for them. I have, indeed, nothing for my own men. They have been living for the last few days principally upon parched corn, and we are badly in need of both rations and forage. I telegraphed to Lynchburg, directing several trainloads of rations to be sent on by rail from there, and when they arrive I should be glad to have the present wants of my men supplied from them."

At this remark all eyes turned toward Sheridan, for he had captured these trains with his cavalry the night before, near Appomattox Station. General Grant replied: "I should like to have our men sent within our lines as soon as possible. I will take steps at once to have your army supplied with rations, but I am sorry we have no forage for the animals. We have had to depend upon the country for our supply of forage."

At a little before four o'clock General Lee shook hands with General Grant, bowed to the other officers, and with Colonel Marshall left the room. One after another we followed, and passed out to the porch. Lee signaled to his orderly to bring up his horse, and while the animal was being bridled the general stood on the lowest step and gazed sadly in the direction of the valley beyond where his army lay—now an army of prisoners. He smote his hands together a number of times in an absent sort of a way; seemed not to see the group of Union officers in the yard who rose respectfully at his approach, and appeared unconscious of everything about him. All appreciated the sadness that overwhelmed him, and he had the personal sympathy of everyone who beheld him at this supreme moment of trial. The approach of his horse seemed to recall him from his reverie, and he at once mounted. General Grant now stepped down from the porch, and, moving toward him, saluted him by raising his hat. He was followed in this act of courtesy by all our officers present; Lee raised his hat respectfully, and rode off to break the sad news to the brave fellows whom he had so long commanded.

Susan B. Anthony

JOANNA STRONG AND TOM B. LEONARD

The Nineteenth Amendment to the Constitution, which provides for full women's suffrage, was not ratified until fourteen years after Susan B. Anthony's death in 1906. Nevertheless, her name more than any other is associated with American women's long struggle to vote. Her firm resolve made her one of our greatest examples of political courage.

What the blazes are you doing here?" shouted the man at the big desk. "You women go home about your business. Go home and wash the dishes. And if you don't clear out of here fast, I'll get the cops to put you out!"

Everybody in the store stopped and listened. Some of the men just turned around and sneered. Others looked at the fifteen women mockingly and guffawed. One man piped, "Beat it, youse dames. Your kids are dirty." And at that, every man in the place bellowed with laughter.

But this banter didn't faze the tall, dignified woman who

stood with a piece of paper in her hand at the head of the fourteen other ladies. She didn't budge an inch.

"I've come here to vote for the President of the United States," she said. "He will be my President as well as yours. We are the women who bear the children who will defend this country. We are the women who make your homes, who bake your bread, who rear your sons and give you daughters. We women are citizens of this country just as much as you are, and we insist on voting for the man who is to be the leader of this government."

Her words rang out with the clearness of a bell, and they struck to the heart. No man in the place dared move now. The big man at the desk who had threatened her was turned to stone. And then, in silence and dignity, Susan B. Anthony strode up to the ballot box and dropped into it the paper bearing her vote. Each of the other fourteen women did the same, while every man in the room stood silent and watched.

It was the year 1872. Too long now had women been denied the rights that should naturally be theirs. Too long now had they endured the injustice of an unfair law—a law that made them mere possessions of men.

Women could earn money, but they might not own it. If a woman was married and went to work, every penny she earned became the property of her husband. In 1872, a man was considered complete master of the household. His wife was taken to be incapable of managing her own affairs. She was supposed to be a nitwit unable to think clearly, and therefore the law mercifully protected her by appointing a guardian—a male guardian, of course—over any property that she was lucky enough to possess.

Women like Susan Anthony writhed at this injustice. Susan saw no reason why her sex should be discriminated against. "Why should only men make the laws?" she cried. "Why should men forge the chains that bind us down? No!" she exclaimed. "It is up to us women to fight for our rights." And then she vowed that she would carry on an everlasting battle, as long as the Lord gave her strength to see that women were made equal in the sight of the law.

And fight she did. Susan B. Anthony was America's greatest champion of women's rights. She traveled unceasingly, from one end of the country to the other. She made thousands of speeches, pleading with men, and trying to arouse women to fight for their rights. She wrote hundreds of pamphlets and letters of protest. It was a bitter and difficult struggle that she entered upon, for the people who opposed her did not hesitate to say all kinds of ugly and untrue things about her and her followers. "No decent woman would talk like that. No refined lady would force her way before judges and men's associations and insist on talking. She is vulgar!"

Many women who knew that Susan Anthony was a refined, intelligent, and courageous woman were afraid to say so. They were afraid that *they* would be looked down on. But in time, they grew to love her for trying to help them.

After a while, many housewives gained courage from her example. Then, in great meetings, they joined her by the thousands. Many a man began to change his notions when his wife, inspired by Susan B. Anthony, made him feel ashamed at the unfair treatment accorded women. Slowly the great Susan B. Anthony was undermining the fierce stubbornness of men.

On that important day in 1872, she and her faithful follow-ers cast their first ballots for President. But though the men in the polling place were momentarily moved, their minds were not yet opened. In a few days, Susan was arrested and brought before a judge, accused of having illegally entered a voting booth.

"How do you plead?" asked the judge.

"Guilty!" cried Susan. "Guilty of trying to uproot the slavery in which you men have placed us women. Guilty of trying to make you see that we mothers are as important to this country as are the men. Guilty of trying to lift the standard of woman-hood, so that men may look with pride upon their wives' aware-ness of public affairs."

And then, before the judge could recover from this onslaught, she added, "But, Your Honor, *not* guilty of acting against the Constitution of the United States, which says that no person is to be deprived of equal rights under the law. Equal rights!" she thundered. "How can it be said that we women have equal rights, when it is you and you alone who take upon yourselves the right to make the laws, the right to choose your represen-tatives, the right to send only sons to higher education. You, you blind men, have become slaveholders of your own moth-ers and wives."

The judge was taken aback. Never before had he heard these ideas expressed to him in such a forceful manner. However, the law was the law! The judge spoke quietly, and without much conviction. "I am forced to fine you one hun-dred dollars," he said.

"I will not pay it!" said Susan Anthony. "Mark my words, the law will be changed!" And with that, she strode from the court.

"Shall I follow her and bring her back?" said the court clerk to the judge.

"No, let her go," answered the elderly judge. "I fear that she is right, and that the law will soon be changed."

And Susan did go on, on to further crusades, on across the vast stretches of the United States, proclaiming in every hamlet where her feet trod, her plea for womanhood.

Today, voting by women is an established fact. Women may keep what they earn; and whether married or single, own their own property. It is taken for granted that a woman may go to college and work in any business or profession she may choose. But these rights, enjoyed by the women of today, were secured through the valiant effort of many fighters for women's freedom, such as the great Susan B. Anthony.

The Tower to the Moon

DOMINICAN REPUBLIC FOLKTALE

*Sometimes people with high titles get high notions of themselves, as
we see in this tale from the Dominican Republic. But a title is no guar-
antee of real leadership, even if your name is "king." Serving the inter-
ests of those who follow is the true crown of leadership.*

Long ago there lived an island king who one night, letting
his thoughts drift beyond the sandy shores of his kingdom,
got it into his head that he would like to touch the moon.

"Why not?" he asked himself. "I am king. What I want, I
get. I want to touch the moon."

The next morning he called the chief carpenter in the land
to his court.

"I want you to build me a tower," he commanded. "One tall
enough to reach the moon."

The carpenter's eyes bulged.

"The moon? Did you say the moon?"

"You heard me. The moon. I want to touch the moon. Now
go do it."

The carpenter went and talked it over with all the other carpenters. They scratched their heads and decided his majesty must have been joking, and built nothing at all.

A few days later, the king summoned the chief carpenter back to court.

"I don't see my tower," he barked. "What's taking so long?"

"But Your Majesty," the carpenter cried, "you can't be serious. A tower to the moon? We don't know how."

"I don't care how!" the king yelled. "Just get it done. You have three days. If by that time I have not touched the moon, I hate to think what will happen to you."

The shaken carpenter went back to his friends, and they scratched their heads some more, and drew lines on paper, and racked their brains for an answer. Finally they came up with a plan.

The chief carpenter went back to the king.

"We have an idea that just might work," he said. "But we'll need every box in the kingdom."

"Excellent!" cried the king. "Let it be done!"

He sent out a royal decree that every box on the island be carried to the palace. The people brought them in every shape and size—crates and chests and cases and cartons, shoe boxes, hat boxes, flower boxes, even bread boxes.

Then the carpenter ordered that all the boxes be piled one on top of the other, until there wasn't a single box left. But the tower wasn't high enough to reach the moon.

"We'll have to make more," he told the king.

So another royal decree went out. His majesty ordered all the trees on the island to be chopped down and the timber brought to the palace. The carpenters made more boxes, and stacked them on top of the tower.

"I think it's high enough," the king announced.

The carpenters looked up nervously.

"Perhaps I should go up first," the chief carpenter suggested. "Just to be on the safe side."

"Don't be silly!" the king barked. "This was my idea. I will be the first one to touch the moon. The honor belongs to me."

He started to climb. Higher and higher he mounted. He left the birds far below, and broke through the clouds. When he got to the top, he stretched out his arms—but he was just barely short! A few more inches, and he would be able to touch the moon! Or at least that's the way it looked to him.

"One more box!" he yelled down. "I need just one more box!"

The carpenters shook their heads. They had already used every stick of wood on the island.

"We don't have any more!" they yelled at the top of their lungs. "No more boxes! You'll have to come down!"

The king stamped his foot and jumped up and down, and the whole tower trembled.

"I won't come down! I won't!" he yelled. "I want to touch the moon, and no one's going to stop me!"

Then his majesty had his brilliant idea.

"Listen here," he called. "I know what to do. Take the first box from the bottom and bring it to the top."

The carpenters stared at each other.

"You fools!" the king yelled. "You're wasting my time! Take out the first box and bring it up now!"

The carpenters shrugged.

"This is a very stubborn king," the chief carpenter said. "I suppose we must obey his command."

So they pulled out the bottom box. You don't need to be told the end of the story.

Acknowledgments

The editor gratefully acknowledges the endeavors of scholars and collectors such as James Baldwin and Jesse Lyman Hurlbut, who in a past age devoted their energies to preserving some of the best of our heritage, and whose works have supplied this volume with many truly great stories.

Reasonable care has been taken to trace ownership and, when necessary, obtain permission for each selection included.

William J. Bennett served as Director of the Office of National Drug Control Policy under President George Bush and as Secretary of Education and Chairman of the National Endowment for the Humanities under President Reagan. He holds a bachelor of arts degree in philosophy from Williams College, a doctorate in political philosophy from the University of Texas, and a law degree from Harvard. Dr. Bennett is currently a codirector of Empower America, and a Distinguished Fellow in Cultural Policy Studies at the Heritage Foundation. He is also chairman and cofounder of K12, an Internet-based elementary and secondary school. He, his wife Elayne, and their two sons, John and Joseph, live in Chevy Chase, Maryland.

A collection of timeless stories that will take you back to early lessons of life and love.

William J. Bennett's *The Book of Virtues* and *The Moral Compass* have quickly become classics—thanks to their homespun truth, traditional values, and moral ideals. Focusing on equality, integrity, and generosity—traits often lost in today's self-centered, cynical society—this collection of favorite stories, anecdotes, and legends reminds us that no matter where we go, a part of us will always be home.